Neston and Parkgate

by

Jeffrey Pearson

Front Cover Design, "Neston Ladies Walk", by David Scott, the Neston Artist. Drawn in 1965 this picture represents a typical Ladies Walk in Neston, when, on the first Thursday each June the members of the Neston Female Friendly Society (founded 1814) walk in procession to a service at the Parish Church carrying staffs dressed with flowers led by their banner and a band.

Parkgate Packet Jug. Made about 1785 this jug bears the legend. "Success to the Parkgate Packets", and what is believed to be an authentic picture of the five packet boats which sailed between Parkgate and Dublin in the later eighteenth century.(Courtesy Merseyside County Museums).

CONTENTS

APPENDICES

ACKNOWLEDGEMENTS

I should like to thank the many people who have furnished me with information, or helped me in any other way, to write this book.

I dedicate this book to the memory of
IAN ROBERT WILLIAMS, R.N.
a Neston man who died in the Falkland War at the age of twenty-one.

First printed in 1985.
Reprinted in 1987.

First published 1985 by Countyvise Limited, 1 & 3 Grove Road, Rock Ferry, Birkenhead, Wirral, Merseyside L42 3XS .... ISBN 0 907768 06 7

Photoset and printed by Birkenhead Press Limited, 1 & 3 Grove Road Rock Ferry, Birkenhead, Wirral, Merseyside L42 3XS.

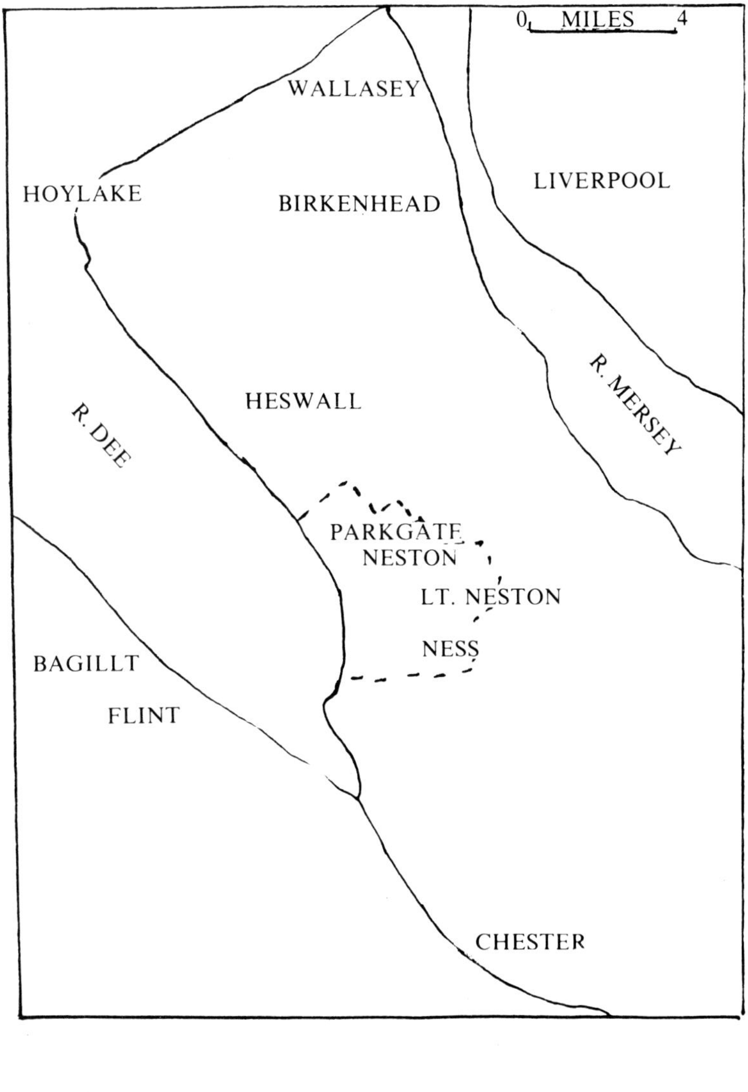

Sketch map to show the location of the Neston-Parkgate area.

INTRODUCTION

There is no place on the Wirral Peninsula with a more interesting history than Neston-cum-Parkgate, as it is labelled on some editions of the Ordnance Survey Map.

In the following pages I have written an outline of that history, devoting the main part of the book to a chronological account of Neston's changing fortunes over the centuries, and the appendices to a consideration of various topics that can be examined more clearly in isolation than in the broad sweep of a chronological account.

All written histories must end at some, more or less, arbitrary date, and I have chosen to conclude this one at 1974, when the old Neston and Ellesmere Port authorities were merged to form the new district authority which is now known as the Borough of Ellesmere Port and Neston. Only in the case of Appendix E, dealing with Ness Gardens, have I deliberately overshot this mark, to give some account of the many important developments that have taken place at the Gardens in recent years.

Inevitably, I shall have omitted much that may be considered by some local historians to be important. I can but remind them that all histories are selective and owe much to the individual perceptions of their authors. It is in the nature of the exercise.

CHAPTER ONE

The Early Years

Neston Cross in the mid-"1960s". (Courtesy Guyse Williams).

Neston is generally believed to have been a Saxon settlement. The first syllable of the name, "nes", is derived from the Anglo-Saxon word for a headland "nesse" or "naze" and "ton" is a typical Saxon ending for a township.

So Neston was "the township by the headland". Inappropriate as this name may now seem to be, the headland certainly existed. Speed's map of Cheshire, dated 1617, shows a clear promentary jutting into the Dee Estuary from a point close to the village, and vestiges of it are marked on Denham's chart of the Dee published in 1839. Almost certainly, over the course of the years, it was eroded to nothing by the continual action of the tides.

There seem to have been two main considerations that influenced the early settlers to choose this particular site. First, it was a place where the underlying sandstone was exposed, providing a solid foundation on which to build. Little Neston and Ness were built on similar drypoint sites. The second consideration was the existence of a potential water supply in the form of a nearby small stream. This stream, which was also used by the early inhabitants of Little Neston, may still be seen running through the Park. Another stream at Ness supplied that settlement.

Some fragments of a grave cross excavated when the old church was being demolished in 1874, suggest that there was some degree of co-operation and cultural cross-fertilisation at some period between the Saxon and Irish-Norse settlements of the Peninsula. While the carvings on the stones are essentially Saxon in character, Irish-Norse influences are obvious. For example, the figure of a priest depicted on one of the fragments is shown clutching a typically Irish-Norse "budget" or book satchel in his left hand.

The first known documentary reference to Neston occurs in the Domesday Book, the great catalogue of England that was compiled in 1085 by order of William the Conqueror. This survey states that the population of Little Neston was eight, and, curiously, that a further eight people lived in two-thirds of the Neston area. No figure is given for that third which was owned by the Church. Domesday also records a priest living at Neston, one of only four in the whole of Wirral, but there is no mention of a church building.

That there was a church on the site in 1180 is certain. The Chronicle of St. Werburgh states that in 1180 the dying Ralph Montalt, Baron of Mold, presented Neston Church to St. Werburgh's Abbey in Chester "..... because of my evil deeds".

Unfortunately for the Abbey, Ralph's action was resented by his nephew Roger de Montalt, Chief Justice of Chester. An entry in the Chronicle, dated 1258, records that Roger entered Neston Church with a body of armed men and turned out the monks who had been sent from the Abbey to perform the services. He then gave the living to his own nephew Ralph.

When, however, the Abbot offered him a manor in return for the living, Roger promptly retrieved it from his nephew and closed the bargain.

The Abbey authorities were nothing if not vindictive. The Chronicler concludes his account of the affair by listing the misfortunes that befell Roger, as a warning to other would-be robbers of the Church. He relates that his eldest son died within fifteen days, and that Roger himself "..... died in poverty within two years, the common people being ignorant of the place of his burial".

The living of Neston Church remained in the hands of the Abbot until the Dissolution of the Monasteries, when it passed into the authority of the Dean and Chapter of Chester Cathedral.

From Chester City Records it is clear that Neston, like a number of other settlements along the Dee coast, was used as an occasional anchorage during the Middle Ages. In the earliest years this seems to have been because the vessels concerned were too heavily laden to reach the City's wharves; in the later years silting choked the approaches to Chester. While a ship's arrival was probably something of an event for the locals, the sight of a fleet of some sixty vessels anchoring off Neston in 1282 must have caused a sensation. Despatched from the Cinque Ports to assist King Edward I to crush a Welsh uprising led by David ap Gruffydd, the fleet lay off Neston for several days while the soldiers who arrived in boats from Chester embarked and then set sail for Anglesey.

To these isolated glimpses of medieval Neston may be added the inferences that it was an essentially agricultural settlement, and that it was a place of some local importance.

That Neston was an argicultural settlement may be deduced from the earliest surviving plan, drawn for the Mostyn estate in 1732, which bears unmistakable evidence of an extensive medieval open-field system.

That is was a place of local importance may be inferred from the fact that it was the centre of a parish which included no fewer than eight townships: Great and Little Neston, Ness, Raby, Leighton, Ledsham, Thornton Hough and Willaston. It was to Neston that the inhabitants of this extensive area were obliged to come for baptisms, weddings, funerals, and any other business demanded by the Church's customs and Calendar. It was to Neston that the officials of the Abbey would have to come when their duties obliged them to visit their parishes.

Little more is known about medieval Neston. It is a place almost covered by the mists of historical obscurity: something can be seen, but the bulk lies hidden.

Parkgate Parade c1960. One of the rare days when the tide reached the sea wall. (Courtesy Guyse Williams).

CHAPTER TWO

The New Quay

The mists of historical obscurity finally cleared from Neston during the sixteenth century, when a quay to handle Chester's shipping trade was built close to the village.

Much of the interest aroused by the construction and business of this "New Quay" or "New Haven", as it was called, was recorded in various documents, which, together convey an impression of Elizabethan/Jacobean Neston as being a bustling, prosperous and rapidly-expanding town.

The construction of the quay represented an attempt by certain Chester merchants to protect their seaborne trade, which was threatened by silting. From Norman times the approaches to the Port of Chester had become increasingly difficult, and masters of vessels that were too large or too heavily-laden to reach the City's wharves had been obliged to anchor at places on the Wirral coast, such as Shotwick, Burton and Neston, where there were no proper facilities for handling their cargoes.

The Old Quay House. (Author's Collection).

The basic problem was the poor scour of the river. Dee tides flow rapidly but ebb slowly. The fast-moving flood carries with it a heavy load of silt, which is allowed to settle on the bed of the estuary by the sluggish ebb. The layers of mud spread by successive tides gradually blocked the approaches to Chester until, in 1540, the city merchants, convinced that they were facing a crisis, petitioned the King's Council to grant them help to build a new quay at Neston.

The site selected for the quay was about a half a mile to the south-west of Neston at a place called "Lightfoot's Pole". The reasons for this choice appear to have been the shelter offered by the naze or promentory that existed there, and the deep water that was found close inshore at this point. Although no contemporary survey records now exist, when the royal hydrographer, Captain Grenville Collins, conducted a survey of the Dee between 1684 and 1689 i.e. some 150 years later when the river was presumably much shallower, he recorded the depth of water thereabouts as being between thirty and forty feet at spring tides.

Work on the construction of the quay began about 1545. It was both slow and money-consuming. The original costing seem to have been completely inadequate because some ten years later the merchants were again obliged to seek help from central government, which responded by ordering special collections towards the cost of the quay to be made in churches throughout the country. Even so, the work dragged on for a further half century. As late as 1598 Chester City Council was so concerned about the lack of progress that it appointed a former Sheriff of the City, John Middleton, to be overseer of the work; he was to see that the labourers worked well and did not waste time, and his expenses were to be met by the City.

It may well have been, however, that the root cause of the problems which dogged the work lay with the engineers rather than the labourers. An examination of Boydell's map of 1771, which shows the quay jutting directly out into the river from the point of the Naze, suggests the possibility that the project was basically ill-considered. To construct a massive stone wall out into the river at a point where the tides flowed at their strongest and which was completely exposed to the winter gales was not something that could be done without great difficulty and expense.

Despite these problems, large quantities of merchandise and a considerable number of passengers passed over the quay, while it was still being built, and later.

Writing in 1615, William Webb referred to Neston in the following terms:

"The well-known town, parish, church and port of Great Neston and the usual place where our passengers into Ireland do so often lie waiting the leisure of the winds, which make many people better acquainted with this place than they desire to be, though there be wanting no

convenient entertainment, if no other want lie in the way; and here is the station of the ships called "The New Quay", where they embark and disembark both men, horses, kine and all other commodities on the back of this Neston."

(King's Vale Royal by William Webb).

Although it was another century before the incumbents of Neston started to record the occupations of those whose names they entered in the Parish Registers, it seems reasonable to deduce from Webb's comments that in his time the town was thriving by providing accommodation and services for the passengers who were waiting to embark for Ireland.

In addition to the Irish trade, a significant amount of commerce was conducted with the Baltic states, which supplied such commodities as timber, pitch and fish, and with the wine exporting countries of France and Spain.

Regular, important, outward cargoes included salt and tanned calves' skins.

Much of the freight which was destined for Chester was transhipped to small vessels to complete the up-river journey to the City, while passengers disembarked to continue by coach. The overland route to Chester passed through Little Neston, Ness and Burton, and then to Shotwick, either by a track through Puddington or by a path which went down to the edge of the river and came out just below Shotwick church, traces of which can still be seen. After crossing the creek at Shotwick the traveller could either follow the old military road through the Park and King's Wood, or take a shorter, but somewhat more hazardous route along the sands.

The tonnage of Dee ships seldom exceeded 100 tons displacement, and few of the Neston ships exceeded 80 tons.

The names of many of the local ships and shipowners are recorded in Chester City archives. For example, in 1571 licences to sail from the Port of Chester (which included the New Quay) to certain other specified ports were granted on the 23rd and 25th May by the Mayor, Sir Lawrence Smith, to the following vessels:

"Richard Bennett of Neston and Wm Waley of the same: "The Trinitie of Neston," which belongeth to the aforesaid Richard."

"William Waley of Neston and Richard Bennett of the same: "The Marten of Neston," which belongeth to the aforesaid William."

"Roger Garrett of Neston and John Lawnsley of the same: "The Katherine of Neston," which belongeth to the aforesaid John."

In July 1588, when the country was awaiting the expected attack by the Armada, the Quay became the centre of an invasion scare. A rumour reached Chester one night that "London and Bristow (Bristol) were set on fire by the Papists and that there were a navye of 700

Spanyards shippes landed at New Quay in Worral, which sudden news raised up all the citizens and cuntrie".

By the early part of the next century the merchants seemed to have decided that their plans had been too ambitious because in 1608 a decree was issued for, "pulling down one half of a certain quay or harbour for shippes called the New Quay".

During the years that followed silting made access to the Quay increasingly difficult, and ships began to anchor a mile further downstream at Parkgate. Gradually the Quay fell into disuse. Equally gradually, common usuage changed its name from "The New Quay" to "The Old Quay", a name that was adopted by cartographers from John Mackay in 1732 onwards.

The ruins of the quay were sold by the city merchants to Sir Roger Mostyn in 1799 and, according to local tradition, many of the stone blocks were used to build the present sea wall at Parkgate.

Until 1943 a building known locally as "The Old Quay House" stood as the last substantial relic of the Haven. Built as a customs house for the "New Quay", in the course of its long history it also served as a prison for runaway servants and as a private dwelling. Unoccupied for the last forty years of its existence, gaunt and eerie in its isolation by the marshes, the building was a magnet to the local children, who were attracted by the spine-tingling legends that had gathered round it. Gradually, the structure deteriorated to the point where it was judged to be dangerous and reduced to the safe heap of rubble that may be seen today, with Home Guard hand grenades.

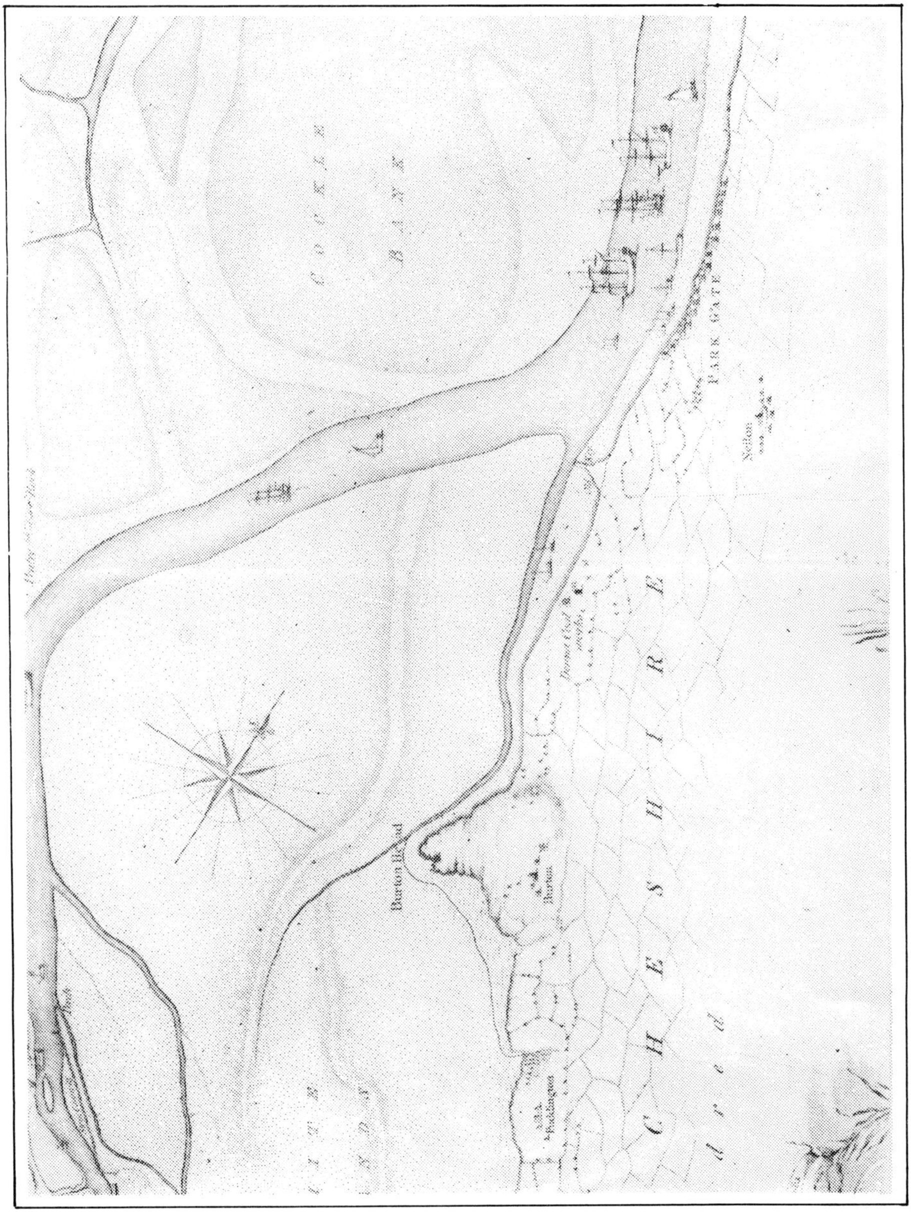

Extract from Boydell's Map of 1771. (Kind permission of Clwyd Record Office).

CHAPTER THREE

The Boom

Taking its name from its proximity to the gates of Neston Park, a deerpark which has long since disappeared, Parkgate developed from being an insignificant hamlet in the early seventeenth century to become the principal port for Ireland.

It seems probable that the anchorage developed because it possessed the advantages of deeper water than that found at the steadily-silting New Quay, while still being close enough to Neston for the ship owners to benefit from the facilities which were available there for the convenience of passengers and the handling of goods. Among the diverse service occupations listed in the eighteenth century Parish Registers were those of carriers, inn-keepers, tailors, shoemakers, barbers, chaisemen, apothecaries, chirurgeons (doctors), an attorney-at-law and at least one pawnbroker. In addition to offering these services, Neston was a market town where supplies could be readily obtained for victualling the ships.

During the seventeenth and eighteenth centuries thousands of passengers made the 120 mile journey to or from Dublin in the two-masted schooners that were used to provide the service. Large quantities of goods were also carried both on the packet boats and in specialised cargo ships, livestock being a particularly important import. With a favourable wind the passage could be made in about fifteen hours, but it often took longer.

Among the passengers who used the port were many distinguished figures. Handel disembarked there in 1742 on his return from Dublin, where he had conducted the first performance of "Messiah". John Wesley often passed through Parkgate on his preaching journeys to and from Ireland, and several references to it may be found in his 'Journal'.

The eighteenth century was nothing less than a boom time for Neston and Parkgate, and some fine houses were built in both places for the merchants and professional men who settled there.

Inns (at one time there were eighteen of them) were also built at Parkgate to accommodate travellers who were waiting for the Dublin packet or the Chester coach. Understandably, if there was to be a delay, many passengers would prefer to wait at Chester rather than at Parkgate and well-known local historian Geoffrey Place, has unearthed a bitter comment made by a traveller in the "1740's", who had been lured from Chester to Parkgate by the false report of a fair wind: "I have learned at Parkgate, that it is a common custom of the publicans there to send up false intelligence to Chester; that the company may come down to lie under the long lash of their bills".

Old cottages at Parkgate. The one nearest to the River, "Dover Cottage" is said to be the one where Emma Hart (neeé Lyon), the future Lady Hamilton stayed in June 1784. (Author's collection).

A more satisfactory link between Parkgate and Chester than the old route along the edge of the Dee was established with the opening of a turnpike road in 1787. As might be expected, this road reached Parkgate via Neston Cross. Another turnpike road connected Neston to the villages of Birkenhead and Tranmere and the Mersey ferries. These important roads, together with the Irish Packet Service and the ferry services that connected Parkgate with Bagillt and Flint on the North Wales coast, established Neston as the main communications centre on the Peninsula. It was a period when contemporary Gazetteers indicated the position of all other towns and villages on Wirral by describing them as being: "situated at . . . miles from Great Neston".

About the middle of the century, when sea bathing became fashionable, Parkgate gradually assumed an additional role: that of a holiday resort. Indeed, it became one of the best-known bathing places in the country.

A letter written in 1754 by a Mrs. Delaney of Dublin described Parkgate as a most agreeable spot: "Such a constant moving picture of ships, sea plants on the beach, seaweed and beautiful shells".

In 1784 the village was visited by Mrs. Hart, who was later to achieve fame as Lady Hamilton, Nelson's mistress. A local woman, born a blacksmith's daughter at Ness some twenty-one years previously, Emma Hart, neé Lyon, returned from her matrimonial home in London to treat a skin complaint from which she was suffering by bathing in sea water. It is said that she stayed in Dover Cottage, which is the last house in Station Road nearest to the sea front.

Balcony House. The former Assembly Room Building and centre of Parkgate's social life. (Author's collection).

Other distinguished visitors to the resort included Mrs. Fitzherbert, the first wife of the Prince Regent and the great J.M.W. Turner.

Mrs. Fitzherbert is said to have spent a number of holidays at Parkgate. On one occasion she discovered that about 700 soldiers were camped nearby, waiting for the troopships that were to take them to Ireland. Hearing that their food was poor, she paid for them to receive an additional daily ration of a quarter of sheep and a measure of potatoes (whatever that may have been) for every seven men.

JOSEPH MANLOVE
OF THE GEORGE INN, PARKGATE,
INFORMS THE LADIES, GENTLEMEN, AND OTHERS THAT,
FOR THEIR BETTER ACCOMMODATION DURING THE BATHING SEASON,
HE HAS PURCHASED AN ADDITIONAL
BATHING MACHINE
ON AN ENTIRELY MODERN CONSTRUCTION,
IN WHICH LADIES MAY BATHE
WITH THE UTMOST EASE AND **SECRECY.**

PRICE FOR A SINGLE BATHING, 8d,
AND EVERY LADY WILL (IF DESIRED)
BE ATTENDED WITH A FEMALE SERVANT

Advertisement from "Chester Chronicle" dated 10th May, 1782.

Local tradition holds that it was at Parkgate that Turner painted some of his glorious sunsets, but there seems to be no proof of this. It is certain, however, that Turner visited Parkgate. This was established by the late Norman Ellison, a local naturalist and writer, who discovered an engraving from a Turner dated 1794 in an old volume of "The Copper Plate Magazine and the Itinerant". Entitled "Flint from Parkgate", it depicts a farm with a field of stooked corn, and two figures with dogs in the Wirral foreground, several ships in sail on the Dee, and Flint Castle and the Welsh Hills in the background.

Richard Ayton, in a book which described a journey he made round the country in the summer of 1813, "A Voyage Round Great Britain", recorded his impression of Parkgate when he arrived there by ferry boat from Wales in the following terms:

". . . the little town of Parkgate, whose single row of houses, gaily dressed in whitewash and red ochre, may be seen and admired from afar. We landed again in our native land at this place, and in our walk from the boat to the inn had an opportunity of seeing all that it holds out to the curiosity and amusement of a stranger. It was built solely for bathers, but has the misfortune to be in the worst situation that could be desired for their accommodation. We are generally content in these kinds of establishments to give up all other conveniences for the sake of salt water, but here that is given up too for two-thirds of a day, and in exchange for it one has the satisfaction of seeing from every window of his house a dismal waste of sand, and that too, so soft and so intersected by deep furrows, that it is not passable with comfort or safety by man or horse. One may reckon, indeed, with certainty on a dip every day, but it is exceedingly annoying to be remodelling your engagements and inclinations according to irregularity of the tide's attendance. The condition of visitors at low water is truly deplorable, but having lingered through the full penance of the ebb tide, their spirits rise with the flood, and at high water there is a general burst of business and animation. We arrived at just such a juncture, when the beach was all alive, and discovered a spectacle which a foreigner might have moralised upon with more seriousness than we of this free country can be permitted to do. Few of either sex thought it necessary to hide themselves under the awnings of bathing machines: posts with ropes fastened to them are fixed in the sands, and these were taken possession of by numerous groups of women, six or seven in a row, jumping, shouting, laughing and screaming, evidently as careless of being seen as of being drowned."

Without doubt, the most enduring of the amenitities provided for the fashionable people who came to stay at Parkgate is the sea wall, which was built as a promenade. It was never a quay. Although Parkgate was a busy anchorage throughout the eighteenth century no quay or jetty was constructed to facilitate the handling of traffic. Ships anchored in the main channel, some hundred yards or so from the beach, and passengers and goods were rowed ashore.

Old photograph of the Middle Slipway and Watch House, Parkgate. From 1799 to 1828 , the Watch House was used as a look-out by Customs Officers.
(Author's Collection).

The first part of the wall to be built was the middle section, from the Watch House to the bulge in the wall, which today encloses that part of the Parade known as "The Donkey Stand". The wall bulged at that point to skirt a tall, narrow building that stood there. Built originally as a customs house, it became Parkgate's first Assembly Building about 1780. This first section of the wall was built about 1810.

The Assembly House was the social centre of the resort, where visitors met to dance and play cards. After it had been converted into sea-water baths in 1812, a new Assembly Room was opened in the building now known as Balcony House.

Among the other places of entertainment were a theatre, a billiard room, several coffee shops, and a racecourse, which was situated on the land now occupied by Parks Field, The Springcroft Estate, and that section of The Wirral Way that lies between them.

The south end of the sea wall from the Donkey Stand to the South Slipway was built about 1830 , and the northern section from the Watch House to the North Slipway was built in the "1840's".

The Ropewalk seems to have been laid about 1814, as a promenade for visitors to use when the weather was too rough for them to stroll on the Parade.

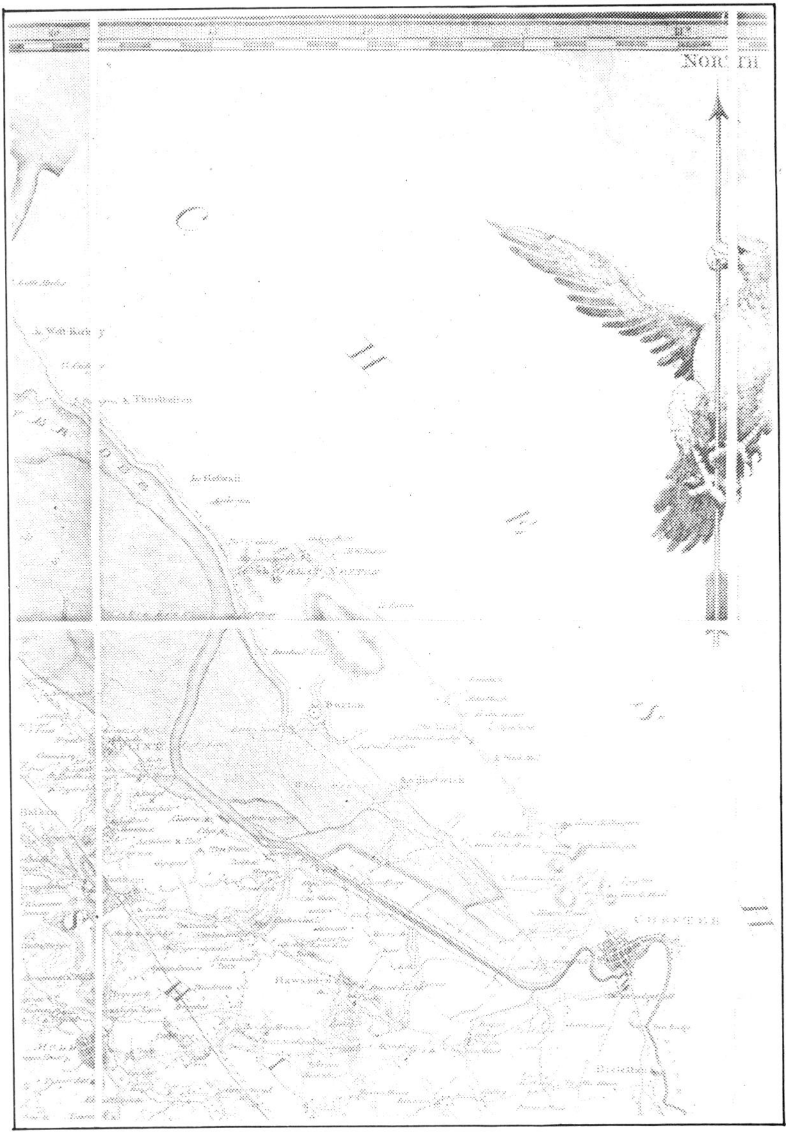

Extract from John Evans's Map of the Dee Estuary (1795). Note how the canalisation of the River between Chester and New Quay (Connah's Quay) had begun to force the main channel over to the Welsh Coast. (Kind permission of Clwyd Record Office).

As if Parkgate did not offer enough opportunities for honest employment, smuggling appears to have been rife. During the eighteenth century customs duties were generally high, and handsome profits could be made by dealing in contraband goods. Like other Wirral anchorages, Parkgate was well-placed to receive cargoes that were run over from the Isle of Man in the fast, shallow-draught, vessels that were specially built there for the purpose. Manx customs duties were much lower than those on the mainland, and the Island prospered by providing goods and services to smugglers.

The cavities which exist in the walls of some older Parkgate houses are said to have been hiding places for contraband, and — irony of ironies — the Old Quay House, a former customs building, is commonly believed to have become a smugglers' lair at this period.

The excise officers were energetic in their efforts to counter these activities, but in one case at least they did not have to exert themselves. A gale in the "1760's" smashed the rudder of a smuggler's lugger and deposited the vessel complete with crew and illicit cargo of salt, on the foreshore immediately under the windows of the Customs House, which stood on part of the "Old Quay" Inn car park.

Because the Customs Building was not situated in a good position from which to maintain a surveillance of the Estuary, the Revenue Service leased the Watch House, by the Middle Slipway, as an observation post in 1799.

In addition to the large scale operations involving gangs, much small scale smuggling seems to have taken place. The Chester Quarter Session Records, for example, include an account of a case in which one Charles Lucas, a seaman on the Dublin Packet, was found guilty of attempting to smuggle forty-six parcels of soap into the country, and of attempting to retrieve them by force after they had been seized by two Parkgate customs men, William Briscoe and William Saunders. It appears that the customs men, having found the soap on the ship, brought it ashore and loaded it on to a horse-drawn cart. They then took it to the Customs House, but before they could start to unload it, Lucas dashed round the corner of the building armed with a cudgel. Pushing the customs men aside, he leapt on to the cart and tried to whip the horses into a gallop. Unfortunately, the records do not go on to describe the manner in which the excise men arrested their assailant.

Some idea of the range of commodities involved in the illegal trade may be gained from the lists of confiscated goods that were offered in the regular sales at the Customs House. They included: brandy, rum, geneva, rectified spirits of wine, starch, hair powder, soap, cotton, linen and vinegar.

Then, quite suddenly, in the early nineteenth century, the great days came to an end. Continued silting made access to the anchorage increasingly difficult for the packets, and the service was transferred to Liverpool, with the Irish trade being finally lost to Chester. Ironically, it was an attempt to increase Chester's waterborne trade that hastened the blow. Between 1732 and 1737 the ten miles of river below Chester had been canalised to allow barges to reach the city. Although the scheme was successful as far as its objective was concerned, it had the effect of diverting the course of the river, from its natural channel on the Wirral side to the Welsh side of the Estuary, thereby accelerating the silting process at Parkgate. The date when the last packet sailed from Parkgate does not seem to have been recorded. Philip Sulley, writing in the late "1880's", when the event still lay within living memory, stated that it was in 1820, but "Paterson's Roads" published in 1829, had still advised travellers that four packets sailed from Parkgate to Ireland every week.

There seems to have been a close relationship between the packet service and Parkgate's standing as a fashionable resort. Possibly it was the sight of the rich and famous passing through the village that attracted the holidaymakers. Perhaps some travellers took the oppportunity of spending a few days at Parkgate before resuming their journeys. Whatever the reason, the number of holidaymakers fell steadily in the years that followed the discontinuation of the service.

Even smuggling ceased to be profitable. At about the same time that the packet service ended the government abolished almost all customs duties, thereby undermining the basis of the smuggling racket.

CHAPTER FOUR

The Slump

The forty years or so that followed the discontinuation of the packet service saw a rapid deterioration in the fortunes of the Neston area. It was a period when the loss of the town's most important function, that of a port and communications centre, plunged the area into a local slump.

Almost inevitably, as soon as the last packet boat had left Parkgate those who were seeking an outlet from Wirral to the sea began to look towards the Mersey and Birkenhead.

In 1835 the New Chester Road was opened, providing a direct link along the north coast of the Peninsula between Chester and Birkenhead, and eliminating the need for passengers travelling between these places to pass through Neston. Little more than a hamlet at the beginning of the century, by the time that plans for Wirral's first railway were being considered, in the "1830's", Birkenhead was a rapidly-expanding commercial and shipbuilding town connected to Liverpool by a steam ferry, which had been operating since 1817, while Neston had already lost most of its former importance. It is not surprising, therefore, that the railway was built between Chester and Birkenhead. The new routes deprived the coach services between Chester and Neston, and Neston and Birkenhead of most of their traffic and by 1850 they had ceased to exist.

An idea of the way in which Birkenhead displaced Neston as the most important town on Wirral can be gained from a glance at the population returns for 1801 and 1851.

	1801	**1851**
Neston area	2,353	3,578
Birkenhead	110	24,285

The fashionable visitors deserted Parkgate almost as soon as the packet service ended. Suddenly, the Village was transformed from being a sophisticated watering-place of national standing to being an obscure local resort, which declined steadily throughout the years that followed. Within a short time the Assembly Room, the theatre, and many of the hotels, closed.

Remarkably, the biggest of the hotels survived until 1855 under the management of a Mrs. Esther Briscoe. A building now incorporated into Mostyn House School, "The George" had flourished in Parkgate's heyday, with its landlords having a wide range of business interests in the resort, including the rental of bathing machines and

Photograph of 1880. The building in the foreground was "The George" inn during the eighteenth and early nineteenth centuries. From 1819 to 1855 it remained in business as the Mostyn Arms Hotel under the proprietorship of Mrs. Esther Briscoe. The building survives as part of Mostyn House School but its facade has been altered. (Collection of Ian Boumphrey).

the provision of a ferry service to Flint. As an establishment which had been designed to cater for the very specialised trade which Parkgate had lost "The George" might have seemed to be particularly vulnerable, but the widowed Mrs. Briscoe refused to be dismayed. With her resolution possibly stiffened by the fact that she had invested a considerable sum in extending and refurbishing the old inn before re-opening it as "The Mostyn Arms" Hotel in 1819, she managed it with such skill and determination that it remained a profitable concern until her death.

The Neston area's economic problems were aggravated by a sudden and coincidental collapse in the local fishing industry.

During the eighteenth and early nineteenth centuries vast quantites of herrings had been landed and cured at Parkgate, but this prosperity came to an end in the "1820's". Mortimer in his book "The History of the Hundred of Wirral" remarked that, "The fisheries at Leighton (for modern purpose Parkgate) were formerly considerable, but are now much neglected".

The first blow to the fisherman fell in 1820, when the bounties which had been payable to herring fishermen since 1750 were discontinued.

About the same time that the bounties were discontinued the fisherman from the ports surrounding the Irish Sea began to face new and formidable competition from Cornish fisherman who operated in a more efficient manner than the local men.

Between 1823 and 1835 a slump occurred in the local herring fisheries.

In his book, "A Short History of the Irish Sea Herring Fisheries During the Eighteenth and Nineteenth Centuries", Professor W.C. Smith commented: "Various reasons for the falling-off were given, including trawling on the spawning beds, beginning the season too early, and shooting the nets before sunset. The strange boats which happened to have commenced exploiting the fisheries in 1823 were, of course, blamed for the evil misfortune".

By 1841, of 235 employed adults in the village only 13 were fishermen.

The Ness Mine remained working (see Appendix B) but it seems to have brought small benefit to the area generally.

To quote Mortimer again: "The village (Ness) is one of the most miserable in the Hundred, consisting of a mere mass of hovels, inhabited by the colliers".

Possibly the clearest indication of the economic plight of the District between 1830 and 1865 was the discontinuation of Neston Fair, which had been held three times a year on February 2nd, May 1st and September 29th for nearly two centuries, and the weekly market, which had been held at the Cross since it had been authorised by a royal charter granted in 1728.

It was a period when some degree of social, as well as economic, change became apparent.

Among other social changes, Congregationalist, Presbyterian and Roman Catholic congregations were established, thereby extending the breadth of Christian tradition already represented by the Anglican and Methodist churches.

Incidentally, for the Established Church Neston's boom and slump were almost reflected in the ministry of two incumbents who held office during these periods, Prebendary Thomas Ward, Vicar from 1784 to 1828 was an enlightened man, who actively promoted the education and general welfare of his parishoners; his successsor, Archdeacon Unwin Clarke, Vicar from 1828 to 1847, cared little for his spiritual duties, being far more interested in hunting with Sir Thomas Stanley's hounds, and in imposing harsh punishments in his capacity as a magistrate.

In her book "Twixt Mersey and Dee", published in 1897, Mrs. Hilda Gamlin recounts an entertaining anecdote about Clarke.

"He was once on his way to sit in his magisterial capacity when he passed a man with a pedlar's stock. The Archdeacon examined his wares, selected a pair of braces, squabbled over the price and acquired them after splitting the difference. Then he exclaimed 'Now, my man, where is your licence?' High words passed and, at last, the pedlar produced his paper, which was perfectly regular. The clergyman had not expected this, so in an ill-tempered tone he said, 'I don't want your braces; you can have them back for a shilling,' a reduction on his purchase. 'Not likely,' said the man, 'When I can get cartloads for sixpence.' 'Well, you may have them for ninepence.' So the man took them and paid for them and they parted. A woman, who had been watching the transaction told the pedlar the name of the Archdeacon and that he was going to Birkenhead to attend a meeting of magistrates. The man asked her to go with him to Birkenhead, where he took out a summons against the Archdeacon for peddling without a licence, and used the woman as a witness to the sale of the braces for ninepence. He served the summons on him as he sat on the bench, had the case heard there and then, and obtained a conviction with fine and costs."

Parkgate about 1860 from a print of the period originally used as a letter heading design for the old "Pengwern Arms" at Parkgate. (Drawing by David Scott).

One of the most significant events, both economically and socially, to occur during this period was the sale by the Mostyn Family of their lands in the District, together with their other Cheshire lands. The family had owned most of Neston and all of Parkgate since 1672, and had leased almost all of the holdings on an annual basis, which was the general custom in Wirral at the time.

While this system of yearly tenancies may have had some advantages for the landlords, it did nothing to encourage tenants to improve their homes or holdings. Agriculture in Neston seems to have been conducted in a half-hearted manner with small regard to the improved farming methods developed elsewhere in the eighteenth century.

Not only did the sale of the Mostyn lands allow many more residents to own their homes and farms, and provide a potent incentive for them to make improvements, it afforded them a measure of independence and dignity which had not previously been possible. It was a portent of better times ahead.

CHAPTER FIVE

The Coming of the Railway

More than any other single factor it was the coming of the Hooton to Parkgate Railway in 1866 that brought a new prosperity.

The first train on the Hooton to Parkgate Line, opened 1st October, 1866. A painting from an original photograph of the event (now lost) taken at the Moorside Lane bridge, Neston. (Courtesy David Scott).

Its route now familiar as that of the Wirral Country Park, the single track was built as a branch line from the Chester-Birkenhead Railway, which had been opened in 1841, to afford the Railway Company access to the steam coal from the Ness Mine, and with some idea of providing a connection with the Parkgate-North Wales Ferry Service. In the event, the Ferry Service was discontinued before the line became operational. (see Appendix D).

The line ended at Parkgate, with stations at Willaston, Neston and Parkgate. The first Parkgate station stood to the south of Station Road on the site of the present country park picnic area.

Twenty years later the London and North Western and Great Western Joint Board, which had built the Railway, extended it to West Kirby, and Parkgate Station was re-sited on the north side of

One of the last trains at the Moorside Lane bridge, Neston. This lane was closed for passenger traffic on 15th September, 1956 and finally for goods in 1962. (Courtesy David Scott).

the road. The line thus crossed the site of the old Parkgate Racecourse, and it seems probable that it was this development that brought the meetings to an end. Certain it is that they were held well into the second half of the nineteenth century.

It was the coming of the Railway that determined the present residental character of Neston-cum-Parkgate and south-west Wirral generally. Its construction was followed by a rapid growth in the villages along its route, as people who worked in Liverpool or Birkenhead realised that they could now live on the quieter Dee Coast of the Peninsula and commute to work. This growth was reflected in the census returns for the years before and after the line was opened. In the thirty years from 1841 to 1871 the population of the Neston area increased by approximately 9%, but in the following thirty years, those roughly coinciding with the first thirty years of the Railway, the population of the town increased by a staggering 124%. Thereafter there was a fall in the rate of increase, but it remained vigorous until well into the "1970's".

From the time that the line was opened until the last few years of its existence, in the "1950's", daily commuter traffic between Neston, and the other places along the line, and Birkenhead was considerable. Morning trains were timed to connect with the ferry services at Woodside, and any failure to make the connection was the subject to an inquiry.

The advent of the Railway transformed the character of the Neston area, stimulated expansion, and, with its potential for providing rapid access to markets, it kindled resurgences in local farming and fishing.

Not only did the advent of the Railway stimulate the expansion of the Neston area and promote economic activity, it provided the means to meet the needs of the growing population. Before the Second World War the bulk of traffic into and out of the area was carried by rail. Inward traffic included such diverse items as: barrels of beer from Burton-on-Trent, roadstone from the quarries of North Wales, manure from Birkenhead Lairage, and seed potatoes from Scotland. Albert Manning, who worked at Neston from 1923 to 1932, remembers an entire circus, complete with elephants, arriving by rail. Outward traffic included: coal from the Ness Mine, shellfish from Parkgate and livestock.

The local police must have been particularly thankful for the existence of the Railway on 8th April 1880 — Election Day — when there was almost a breakdown in law and order.

It was the first election to have been held in the town for forty years. The sun shone, flags danced in the spring breeze, the church bells rang, and in the streets people flaunted rosettes to proclaim their political allegiances: yellow for Liberal and blue for Conservative. Drink flowed in the pubs.

The possibility of trouble had not been overlooked by the Authorities. An Assistant Superintendent Plant had been drafted from Birkenhead to take charge of police operations for the day and to provide the election experience that the local Sergeant, Jim O'Donnell, and his men lacked.

It proved to have been a wise precaution. At about two o'clock sporadic fighting broke out at various points in the High Street. This early skirmishing appears to have been non-political in character, being occasioned by such gentlemen as Frank McLevy, who threw down his hat and defied all comers to tread on it, and William Millan who accepted the challenge with the words "I will have a go".

At about 2.30 p.m. however, the appearance of a group of men leading a lamb beribboned in Conservative blue from the direction of Parkgate provoked something approaching a crisis.

Within minutes, the brawl that started when they were set upon by Liberal supporters had spread and developed into a street battle involving dozens of individual encounters.

It was with considerable difficulty that the handful of policemen managed to separate the factions and to impose an uneasy truce on the town, but, despite the scale of the fighting they made no arrests, confining themselves to restraining and warning the combatants.

Among those warned was a certain Sarah Mellor, who was found to have an apron full of stones. Although she responded to warnings with obscenities and abuse, it was not until later in the day when she took to embracing policemen with every sign of affection that she was arrested.

Aware that he and his men had won nothing but a breathing space, Plant telegraphed Birkenhead for reinforcements.

Thanks to the co-operation and fast work of the Railway Management, the Police Authorities were able to get thirty extra constables from Birkenhead to Neston within the hour.

They were needed. Throughout the afternoon tension increased steadily, scattered fighting occurred, and a number of arrests were made.

As daylight faded the police found themselves confronted by a howling, stone-throwing rabble, estimated by Plant to number over a thousand.

Drawing their batons, the police charged the rioters, who scattered and retreated to neighbouring alleyways, from where they maintained a steady barrage of missiles on Plant's men. Some broke into nearby gardens and tore branches from trees, the better to come to close quarters with the police.

It was at this point that Assistant Superintendent Plant sent for a local Magistrate, James Corbett, to read the Riot Act - that is, the Act that allowed the Police to call on the Army for assistance.

Fortunately for all concerned, the magistrate arrived during a lull in the fighting that enabled him to address the rioters. Standing at the Cross, brandishing his copy of the Act, he warned them of the serious consequences that could follow if he read it, and appealed to them to go home.

It worked. Slowly at first, and then more and more rapidly, the crowd melted away until the streets were empty. By ten o'clock Plant considered the situation to be stable enough for him to stand down all his men, except for those who would normally be on duty.

Considering the scale of the disturbances, surprisingly few rioters actually appeared in court. Only seven men and one woman were convicted of being drunk and disorderly, and were fined either one pound or ten shillings, according to the gravity of their offences, with the option of fourteen days or seven days hard labour respectively.

The Chairman of the Magistrates on that occasion was Christopher Bushell, in whose honour the fountain monument was erected at the Cross. A Liverpool wine merchant who lived in

Neston, he took a lively interest in local affairs and gave generously to local charities. Among his many good works he sank a public well at the Cross in 1865, and the community expressed its appreciation by raising a subscription to pay for the monument to be placed over the well in 1882. Rather curiously, the fountain did not use the well water; instead it drew on the newly-installed piped water system. In the event, the fountain proved to be temperamental, and the spouts were blocked off after a few years.

Christopher Bushell was also one of the most prominent figures associated with the rebuilding of the Parish Church, being a member of the special Executive Committee and a generous subscriber to the Restoration Fund. Built about 1150, the fabric of the old church had been so weakened by a number of ill-planned alterations over the centuries that it was considered to be unsafe and beyond restoration. Indeed, it may never have been a sound structure because the south wall lacked a proper foundation.

Neston Parish Church, a photograph before the restoration in 1875. (Courtesy David Scott).

In the period 1874-75 the Norman church was demolished and the present, much larger, structure was built to the design of Francis Doyle at a cost of £6,563.18s. 11d. The Vicar, Canon Richard Gleadowe, made use of a small trowel that was discovered in the old masonry to lay the first stone of the present building.

Of the old church only the tower remained, having been restored at the turn of the seventeenth and eighteenth centuries.

The new Church. Built 1875. The new Church is much bigger than the old one. The old tower was retained but embrasures were added. (Collection of David Scott).

Vicar of Neston from 1853 to 1893, Richard Gleadowe, was a remarkable man who combined a burning sense of duty with a solidly practical outlook. Although he was not beyond the occasional lapse into bigotry, his long ministry, was a generally enlightened one, characterised by his indefatigable work on behalf of his flock and the community as a whole. His own interests he considered last.

During the cholera epidemic of September, 1866, for example, Gleadowe made daily visits to comfort those suffering from the disease. Other than Doctor David Russell, he was the only person to go willingly into the plague-stricken houses. The disease raged for a fortnight, during which period it killed thirty-seven people. Local tradition holds that the victims were buried in a mass grave, covered in lime, but the idea of someone collecting the dangerous corpses to bury them together in one grave when the epidemic had passed does seem improbable.

With the cholera threat over for the time being, Russell, Gleadowe, Bushell and several other prominent residents began to plan the only effective defence against further outbreaks: a clean, piped, water supply. Although good water could be obtained from the new public well on the Cross and the many private wells that existed, many Nestonians still used the very doubtful water from the small brooks in the area. The main problem was financial. Only a body authorised to levy a local rate could raise the funds and exercise the powers needed to install an adequate piped water system, and such a body

Neston Cross about 1900. (Collection of Ian Boumphrey).

did not exist. The last vestiges of the old manorial system had vanished from the area with the sale of the Mostyn lands, leaving a serious vacuum in local administration. Fortunately, the means to fill it had been provided by "The Local Government Act" of 1858, which authorised local communities to elect Boards empowered to assume reponsibility for certain matters, such as water supply, drainage, sewage disposal, and street lighting, and, furthermore, to raise a rate to carry out these duties.

Accordingly, a public meeting was organised in March, 1867 to discuss the formation of a Local Board. It was a stormy occasion. Memories of the cholera outbreak had begun to fade, and there were those to whom the prospect of actually paying for a good water supply and a modern sewage system did not appeal. In the event, the proposal to establish the Board was adopted, but there were sections of the community among whom resentment continued to smoulder for years.

The Board met for the first time on 30th August 1867 in the Church School (the present infants' school, next to The Malt Shovel) under the chairmanship of Christopher Bushell and a rate of 6d in the £1 was declared.

In the twenty-seven years of its existence Neston Local Board implemented several important measures which secured a sound basis for the modernisation of the town, including: the construction of a waterworks on the site of the present waterworks in Little Neston; the installation of a sewage plant in a field to the south of Church Lane, still known from the most prominent feature of those early works as "Tanks Field"; and the provision of street lighting.

Parkgate Scene about 1910. Children play on a yawl. (Collection of Ian Boumphrey).

Private enterprise made a contribution to this general modernisation when The Neston and Parkgate Gas Company was formed in 1882, and with the installation of the first telephones by the National Telephone Company in 1889. A third railway station was provided for the area when a new line which had been built from Seacombe to Mold was opened in 1895.

In 1894 the Board was dissolved and replaced by "Neston-cum-Parkgate Urban District Council," a type of authority which had been sanctioned by The Local Government Act of that year.

Under the direction of this new body, Neston bustled its way into the twentieth century with the construction of a modern sewage disposal plant at Moorside in 1902-03, and with the erection of a public library.

Planned as Neston's memorial to Queen Victoria, the Library was built in 1907 on land given by Mrs. Russell, widow of Dr. David Russell, and with the aid of a handsome grant from the American industrialist Andrew Carnegie. With the provision of a library service Neston-cum-Parkgate Council became the smallest library authority in the county, a distinction it retained even when it was reformed, with an extended area of jurisdiction, as "Neston Urban District Council" in 1933.

Several of the area's existing schools, or their direct predecessors, were founded in the second half of the nineteenth century and the first decade of this century. St. Winifred's Roman Catholic School was established in 1857, and in the following years Anglican schools were opened at Neston, Parkgate and Ness Holt. A council school established in 1905 was housed in temporary quarters at Little Neston until the new, purpose-designed buildings on Burton Road were ready in 1909.

The Council School, in Burton Road about 1920. (Courtesy David Scott).

At the outbreak of the First World War Neston offered all the services and amenities that could have reasonably been expected of a town at that time except electricity: for that Nestonians had to wait until 1928.

CHAPTER SIX

1914 - 1945

When the new Wirral Battalion of the Cheshire Regiment mustered at Chester Castle on 5th September, 1914 — just a month after the outbreak of the First World War — there were fourteen men from Neston-Parkgate area in its ranks. Over the following four years a steady stream of men left to serve with the forces, and by the Armistice in 1918, over three hundred local men were wearing, or had worn, the King's Uniform.

For a few months after the outbreak of war there was a lull, during which time those who remained at home could do little but await developments.

Gradually, the ripples of war spread to touch Neston. The news of the first Zeppelin raids in early 1915 created a demand for dark material from which to make black-out curtains, and prompted the Committee of the Female Friendly Society to cancel the Annual Walk for the duration of hostilities.

Like many similar establishments throughout the country, Neston Institute — now the Civic Hall, and Parkgate Convalescent Home were commandeered and converted into temporary military

Parkgate Scene 1916. (Collection of David Scott).

View from the roof of Mostyn House School 1917. (Collection of David Scott).

hospitals. The sight of the blue-trousered patients soon became familiar about the town, and many were welcomed into local homes.

Some of the bigger houses such as "Leighton Court" were converted into small munitions factories where volunteers spent their spare time filling shells.

Army units arrived by train to camp at Parks Field for a few months before leaving on their grim business.

In personal terms, the news from the War Zones was usually bad. One resident commented recently that she remembers that hardly a week passed without news of someone's son or husband being killed or wounded.

In 1918 Neston learned that Christopher Bushell — grandson of the Bushell whose generosity is commemorated by the Cross Monument — had won the Victoria Cross, posthumously.

A Lieutenant-Colonel in the Royal West Surrey Regiment, Christopher Bushell was severely wounded in the head while personally commanding "C" Company of his Division in France. He continued to walk about in front of his troops and refused to have the wound dressed until the line was reorganised in a strong position to meet a turning movement of the enemy. He later died of his wound.

During the course of the First World War Neston lost ninety-one men.

For many Nestonians, as for people elsewhere, the inter war years brought hard times. The local unemployment problem precipitated by the closure of the Ness Mine in 1927, the national crisis of the General Strike, and the international catastrophe of the Slump, were all reflected in a shortage of money and of the necessities that money could buy.

Men stood about the streets hoping for the chance of employment, while their bellies rumbled, their clothes wore thin, and their pride disintegrated. Many of them lived in the slums which still existed in such corners as "Golden Lion Yard", opposite the Town Hall.

Both as individuals and in groups, some of the more fortunate residents tried to help the unfortunate. For example, during the winter months Mrs. Arthur Bulley made frequent visits to Ness Holt School, in her 'Model T' Ford mini-bus, with hot soup for the pupils. At the same time, she would make a mental note of any pupil whose clothes betrayed extraordinary hardship, and then find some diplomatic way to help his or her family.

Although not unknown, grinding proverty of the worst sort was rare. At that time farming was still an important activity in the Neston area, and it still provided a significant amount of such seasonal work as potato picking.

Many and varied were the means whereby some people created work for themselves. Hawking was one such activity. Coal was pushed on handcarts to be sold in the sort of very small quantities that people on hard times might be able to buy. Home-made ice cream was another commodity which was offered for sale in the streets. Almost certainly, however, the most commonly hawked commodity in the area was fish. Parkgate was still a fishing village,

Parkgate beach scene in the "1920s" (Collection of Ian Boumphrey).

and the hawkers would buy the fish from the fishermen, and then push their handcarts all over Wirral to sell it. In those days it was not unusual to see a queue of twenty or more hawkers standing outside a fisherman's door, waiting for him to return with his catch.

A stormy day at Parkgate in the "1920s". (Collection of Ian Boumphrey).

In autumn many of the womenfolk would gather blackberries and mushrooms in the fields, which have now disappeared under housing development, to sell at Birkenhead Market. Unless they were fortunate enough to be offered a lift, they walked all the way there and back.

Of course, such wild crops could always be used by the Nestonians themselves, and those who spent long hours tending their gardens or allotments — as many did — were able to remain largely self-sufficient as far as vegetables were concerned.

When the Neston and Parkgate Housing Association was formed by a group of prosperous residents in 1928 to help to provide decent rented accommodation for those living in squalor, much emphasis was placed on the provision of large gardens to encourage the tenants to grow vegetables and keep hens. By raising interest-free loans from its members and with the help of a government subsidy, the Association was able to build a considerable number of houses on Liverpool Road and on Marshlands Road. Some were provided with half-acre gardens. The Association is still very active, and by building "The Court" off Marshlands Road in the years following the Second World War, it became the first housing concern in Cheshire to provide sheltered accommmodation for the elderly.

Mostyn House pupils sand yatching in the "1920s". (Collection of Ian Boumphrey).

The Council, too, built estates in various parts of the District, and, despite the difficult financial climate, a considerable amount of speculative housing development took place.

It would, therefore, be a mistake to visualise the Neston District as presenting a picture of unrelieved gloom in the inter-war year.

Indeed, Parkgate was enjoying a degree of relative prosperity.

In 1923, the Headmaster of Mostyn House School, A. Grenfell, opened a large open-air swimming pool at the far end of the North Parade, using the sea-water from the Estuary. Although Grenfell built the pool primarily for the benefit of his pupils, he also opened it to the general public. Indeed, he depended on his patrons' money to support it and on one occasion, at least, when receipts fell below his expectations he employed low cunning to restore them: he wrote a letter to the local paper, under a false name, complaining about the indecent swimsuits that had been in evidence at Parkgate Baths during the previous weekend.

It was rarely that he needed to consider such subterfuges. Parkgate Baths were very popular, and on fine days in the summer they drew crowds from miles around. In 1930 Grenfell was able to add a second, children's pool.

Two gastronomic delights that also drew visitors to Parkgate were Nicholl's ice cream and the local shrimps.

There was something very special about the ice cream, that was made by the Thomas family, who presided at Nicholl's. Visitors flocked to buy it and to enjoy the view from the balcony over the shop as they ate it.

Parkgate Baths in the early "1930s". (Collection of Ian Boumphrey).

Parkgate shrimps were — and, to an extent, still are — famous throughout the north-west, with a fame that supported a considerable number of shops and cafes.

For much of the inter-war period there was a good beach for visitors to enjoy, and the wide sandy expanses that stretched for miles in front of the sea wall encouraged some adventurous spirits to build and operate sand yachts.

The great end-of-season attraction was the annual charity fireworks display. Another of Headmaster Grenfell's ideas, it packed the promenade with spectators.

The fireworks were arranged about two hundred yards out on the sandbanks, on a day when the tides would not ruin the show. As dusk fell the School's carillon, played by a Belgian virtuoso invited to Parkgate for the occasion, rang out to invite and entertain the gathering crowd.

When it was dark the show began. It lasted for about an hour and, from all accounts, it was always memorable. While the fireworks played, collectors passed among the crowd soliciting donations for the year's charity.

Although it was the outbreak of the Second World War that brought the fireworks displays to an end, there were clear signs that Parkgate's days as a port and a resort were all but finished. Silting had continued apace. The local fishermen had begun to work from Heswall, only bringing their boats back on the highest tides for painting and other maintenance work. A layer of mud had settled on the sand, and the first tufts of spartina grass had appeared by the

South Slipway. The baths remained open until the early "1950's", when so few tides reached Parkgate that the owners could no longer change the water at frequent intervals.

"An Outline Plan for Neston Urban District", published by Neston Urban District Council in 1946 visualised a future for Parkgate as a "quiet resort", based on the construction of a marine lake, but that proposal has remained nothing more than an idea which is revived from time to time.

The Neston experience in the Second World War must have been very similar to that of many other communities. With the outbreak of hostilities many young men, particularly those in the Territorial Army, were called up, and this continued in the following years with men and women leaving for the War as they reached the age for conscription.

In mid 1940 a few refugee children arrived from the Channel Isles and a very considerable number of evacuees arrived from London, all to be billeted with local families.

Shortly after the beginning of the War, the Government started to build an estate of one-storey hostels on Clayhill to house children evacuated to the area, but by the time the buildings were ready, in 1942, it was considered that the danger of heavy bombing had decreased to the point where the hostels were not needed for their original purpose, and for the remainder of the War they were used as a naval shore establishment, "H.M.S. Mersey". Today the Clayhill Industrial Estate occupies the site.

Two home guards units were formed, one at Neston and the other at Little Neston. Observation posts were established on the Parish Church Tower and on the roof of Mostyn House School by the Neston Platoon, and on the then very high colliery slag heaps and in a specially constructed bunker at the Old Quay by the Little Neston Platoon. Two adjacent shops on the Cross were converted into an Auxilliary Fire Station, and Civil Defence air raid shelters were built at various points in the area.

Again the Committee of the Female Friendly Society suspended the Annual Walk for the duration of the War.

Nestonians heard and saw much of the air attacks on Merseyside, but suffered little themselves. Frequently during the nights of 1940 and 1941, they heard the unmistakable broken rhythm of German aircraft engines passing overhead and frequently they looked northwards to see the sky glowing red as Liverpool and Birkenhead burned. In 1941 a Junkers 88 bomber crashed at Parkgate.

Many enemy planes caught in the box-barrage of anti-aircraft fire surrounding Merseyside jettisoned their bombs anywhere before

Delivering beer to "The Bull and Dog Inn" Bull Hill, Little Neston c1920. (Author's Collection).

making their escape. It was in that way that a few bombs fell on Neston, and several other places in South Wirral.

Of the bombs dropped on Neston, the only one to cause any damage, fell in the garden of William Morrison's house, "Glenton" at the top of Bull Hill, Little Neston, destroying the lawn and shattering the windows of the nearby cottages.

For many there was grief to be borne with the news of a son, husband or friend killed while serving with the forces or the Merchant Navy, and, what was sometimes worse, notification that a loved one was missing. Occasionally sorrow was turned to joy by the news that a long-missing relative was alive. Stanley Bailey was missing for over two years before his wife and mother heard that he was alive and held prisoner by the Japanese.

Late in 1941, Neston again learned that a local man had been awarded the V.C. George Gunn, son of the local doctor, had been posthumously decorated for outstanding gallantry in North Africa. The citation read:

"On November 21, 1941, Second-Lt. Gunn was in command of a troop of four anti-tank guns, part of a battery of twelve guns attached to a rifle brigade column in Side Rezegh.

Under heavy fire from 60 enemy tanks, the battery was almost destroyed, in spite of Second-Lt. Gunn's efforts to re-group and encourage his men. Eventually, only two guns were left in action and were subjected to relentless fire.

Immediately afterwards one of these guns was blown up and the portee of the other set on fire. All the crew were wounded, except the sergeant, although the last gun itself remained undamaged.

Second-Lt. Gunn ran to the emplacement through intense fire and put the gun into action on the burning portee, the sergeant acting as loader. Regardless of the concentrated enemy fire, Second-Lt. Gunn's shooting was so accurate at a distance of 800 yards that at least two enemy tanks were hit and set on fire and three others were badly damaged.

At any monent the fire might have reached the ammunition with which the portee was loaded, but the two men fought on until Second-Lt. Gunn fell dead, the victim of a stray bullet which shattered his forehead."

Twice in 1945 Nestonians danced on the Cross: once following the German surrender, and again when the Japanse capitulated.

Of those who marched away to war 61 failed to return.

CHAPTER VII

A Pleasant Place to Live

Post second World War Council Housing. The Liverpool Road Estate. (Courtesy Alban Knox).

The thirty years, or so, between the end of the Second World War and the merging of Neston and Ellesmere Port local authorities saw a rapid expansion of the Neston area.

Beginning with the Rose Garden Estate at Little Neston in 1947, council and private housing was erected at an average rate of 180 dwellings a year in the "1950's" and "1960's", to meet the needs of a swelling population. It was an expansion that covered the fields that had existed between Neston, Parkgate, Little Neston and Ness, and blurred their separate identities.

Many people employed in the factories and offices of Merseyside found Neston a pleasant place in which to live. Surrounded on three sides by Green Belt Areas — for what they are worth — and overlooking the open spaces of the Dee Estuary to the Clwydian Mountains, it is outside the Merseyside Conurbation and yet conveniently situated for easy travel by car or public transport.

The census returns made during this 30-year post-war period all showed about 55% of the gainfully-occupied population as travelling daily to places outside of the area. Ministry of Labour statistics show that, although some of the remaining 45% of workers were employed in local light industries, the majority were engaged in service occupations connected with the residential character of the district, such as shop work and the various occupations associated with the building trade.

While it was basically the same pattern that had been set by the opening of the Hooton-West Kirby Railway in 1866, the town was no longer dependent on the Railway to carry its commuters and goods. In the period following the War railways in general had begun to lose traffic to the resurgent and expanding road transport industry, and the "1950's", with their spectacular increase in car ownership, saw large numbers of passengers deserting the railways for the roads. Of course, the Hooton-West Kirby line was not immune to these forces. Business declined to the point where it was no longer economic to maintain passenger services, and on 15th September, 1956 the last passenger train ran from West Kirby to Hooton. The Line remained open for the carriage of a shrinking volume of goods until 1962. In 1963 the track was raised and in 1966 both Neston and Parkgate stations were dismantled. The Seacombe Line managed to survive on the iron-ore traffic which was carried from Bidston Dock to Shotton.

Neston (South) Railway Station in 1966. (Author's Collection).

In April 1974 Neston Urban District Council was merged with the Borough of Ellesmere Port in a district authority, which is now known as The Borough of Ellesmere Port and Neston. Although the merger was almost certainly disliked by the majority of Nestonians, it was widely regarded as the price that had to be paid to escape from the danger of being absorbed into the new synthetic, County of Merseyside.

APPENDIX A

The Fishermen of Parkgate

Parkgate Promenade c1890. (Author's Collection).

Today it is difficult to visualise Parkgate as a busy fishing haven, but only fifty years ago some thirty fishermen worked from the village. Silting has been almost unbelievably rapid. Where now the salt march stretches as far as the eye can see, a high tide in the "1930's" could give a depth of five fathoms under a boat's keel.

In those days the visitor might have seen the fishing boats leaving their moorings for a day's work, or returning with a catch of flat fish or shrimps, accompanied by a swirling, screaming, squabbling, cloud of gulls on the look-out for pickings from the net debris being thrown overboard.

He would certainly have seen the sacks of mussels and cockles heaped at the slipways, waiting to be collected and taken to Parkgate Station for delivery to Manchester, Liverpool and other destinations in the industrial north of England. He would have also seen the nets hanging to dry on the railings by the Middle Slipway, and the tables set up outside many of the cottages for the sale of fish.

Group of Parkgate Fisherfolk on Middle Slip c.1890. (Author's Collection).

The brothers James and Christopher Peters are the last fishermen of a family that worked from Parkgate for many generations. Their training for the trade in the early years of this century, supervised by their strict but kindly father John, was nothing less than thorough. While the six girls of the family helped their mother about the house and with the running of the family smallholding, the boys learned to catch and sell fish. There were a surprising variety of skills involved in their trade, including knitting and making up the different kinds of net used, sailing boat maintenance and repairs, and the techniques of the various kinds of fishing.

It was a training that began early. Every weekday morning the older boys who were still at school — those aged about twelve or thirteen — rose at 5.30 a.m. and then took the previous day's catch to Rock Ferry in the family's horse-drawn trap. At Rock Ferry they then handed the fish over to a carrier for transport to Liverpool Market via the Ferry. They then returned home for breakfast before going to school.

The evenings were usually spent shelling shrimps. It was a task which the whole family shared, sitting around the great oil-cloth covered table with a hillock of freshly caught shrimps in the centre. Hour after hour they sat steadily picking the shells away from the pink fish. As the pile in the centre of the table fell, it was replenished from a sack standing nearby.

In mid-winter, when there were no shrimps to catch or when bad weather prevented the boats from going out, the boys were obliged to spend two hours every evening learning to make nets. They learned to knit the netting by hand and then to make up the shrimp and fish trawls and the draught and trammel nets used for taking salmon.

When his sons were old enough to leave school John first took them out in his own boat. He taught them where to find the fish at different times of the year and in different weather conditions and how to catch. When he considered his sons to be competent he bought more boats for them to work.

For many years the traditional Parkgate fishing boat was the yawl. Known locally as 'jigger boats' they were two-masted shallow draught vessels that were particularly well-suited to local conditions.

Parkgate Yawl (Jigger Boat) under sail. (Author's Collection).

About 1900, however, a new type of fishing boat appeared in the Dee Estuary. Technically described as Morecambe Bay Prawners, to the fishermen they were never anything else but 'nobbies'.

Single-masted vessels, which ranged in length from twenty to thirty-five feet, they were characterised by their speed under sail. So fast were they that in the later transitional period when some boats were powered by engine and the others still depended on sail, the sailing boats could always outstrip the power boats if they had a following wind.

Morcambe Bay Prawner (Nobby) under sail. (Courtesy Merseyside Maritime Museum).

The new boats proved so popular with fishermen that over the course of the following thirty years the nobby displaced the jigger boat as the standard Dee fishing boat.

Another type of craft, which was used for the mundane tasks of cockle and mussel gathering, was the large rowing boat that was known locally as a 'punt'. With these boats the fishermen could drift down river on the ebb-tide to the sandbanks and the mud-flats near to the mouth of the estuary where the shell fish beds lay, spend the day raking for shellfish, and return to Parkgate on the next tide.

Those days, in the first three decades of this century, were prosperous time for Parkgate. The now dismantled railway station was always busy with the outward traffic of fish and the inward traffic of ropes, cordage, spars, sails and all the other paraphernalia of the fishermen.

Every Saturday a train of some twenty to thirty trucks, full of shellfish, left the station for destinations in Lancashire and

Unloading shell fish from a punt fitted with a lug sail at the Middle Slip. (Courtesy Ian Boumphrey).

Yorkshire. It is said that at that time Parkgate station took more cash in a week than all the other stations on the Hooton-West Kirby line combined, took in a year.

Parkgate fishing folk were an independent people who took a fierce pride in being their own masters.

At the same time there was a strong community spirit. Never more so than in times of trouble. For Parkgate people, as for fishing folk everywhere, tragedy and death were never far away, and it was in moments of crisis that neighbour drew close to neighbour.

There was, for example, the occasion in 1919 when the boats were caught out in a sudden storm, and struggled through the turmoil and darkness to their moorings with the greatest difficulty.

On the following morning word went round that George (Slen) Mellor, who had been working his boat alone, had failed to return home. A search party which set out to scour the coastline for signs of Slen, found his boat secured to its moorings chain and his body lying on the sandbank beside it. He had, apparently, fallen into the sea and drowned while he was trying to scramble from his yawl and into the punt he used as a tender.

Fate dealt the Mellor family another blow just a year or so later when Slen's seventeen-year-old nephew, his brother's son, also named George, was drowned. He had been working on his father's

Parkgate nobbies fishing off Hilbre c.1920. (Author's Collection).

boat, fishing off Mostyn, when the boom knocked him overboard. Immediately his sea boots filled with water and dragged him down.

His father called to Bill and Fred Higgins, who were trawling nearby in their nobby "Kingfisher", to help him search for the boy. They hauled in their net, preparatory to joining the search, only to find young Mellor's body in it.

But there were happy times, too. The great annual event in the life of the village before The First World War was the Parkgate Fishermen's Regatta, which was held in June or July, according to the suitability of the tides.

For weeks before the event all the talk was of the races and the competitors. From Heswall, Thurstaston, Mostyn, Connah's Quay, and all the other anchorages on the Estuary, fishermen called at Parkgate to hand in their entries.

On the day itself the buildings along the Parade were festooned with flags and bunting, and a band was hired for the occasion.

The first race to be started was always that for nobbies. At that time, of course, the boats were still working under sail, and it was under canvas that they raced. The second race to be start was that for yawls.

Both of these races were held over a triangular course that ran from Parkgate down to Heswall, across the Estuary to Mostyn and

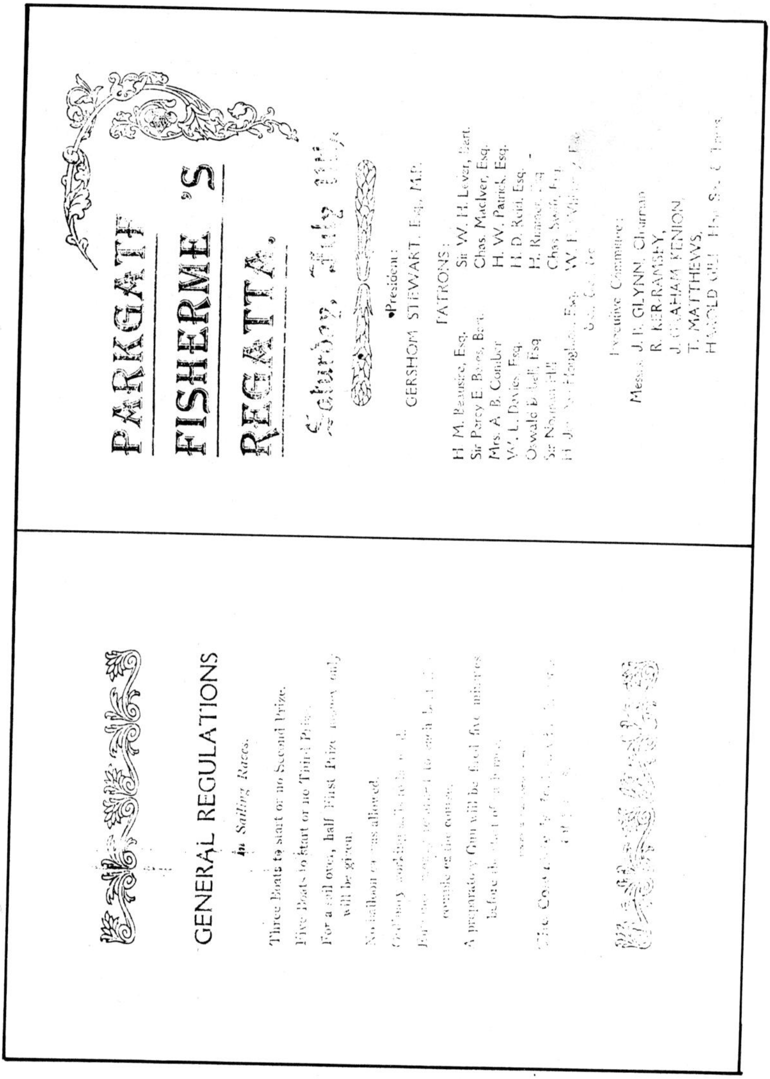
GENERAL REGULATIONS

In Sailing Races.

Three Boats to start or no Second Prize.

Five Boats to start or no Third Prize.

For a sail over, half First Prize money only will be given.

A preparatory Gun will be fired five minutes before the start of each race.

PARKGATE FISHERMEN'S REGATTA,

President:

GERSHOM STEWART, Esq., M.P.

PATRONS:

H. M. Beausire, Esq.
Sir Percy E. Bates, Bart.
Mrs. A. B. Comber
W. L. Davies, Esq.
Sir W. H. Lever, Bart.
Chas. MacIver, Esq.
H. W. Patrick, Esq.
H. D. Reid, Esq.

Executive Committee:

Messrs. J. P. GLYNN, Chairman
R. KER-RAMSEY,
J. GRAHAM KENION,
T. MATTHEWS,
HAROLD GILL, Hon. Sec. & Treas.

Programme cover of the last Parkgate Fishermen's Regatta. (Held in 1914). (Author's Collection).

back to Parkgate, a distance of some 15 miles. It was a course that required competitors to work both with and against the wind and the tide.

While these larger boats were battling it out in the distance, the spectators on the Parade were able to watch the races between the small sailing boats, and the rowing boat races.

The finishes of the nobby and jigger boat races were the high-point of the day.

As the boats drew into sight, eyes were strained to identify the leader, and as the boats approached the finishing buoy, the spectators expressed they encouragement with such unreserved enthusiasm that, immediately after the races, many were obliged to retire to the nearby "Red Lion" to find some comfort for their tortured throats.

So fiercely contested were those events that, despite the length of the course, there were occasions when the winning boat and the second were separated by no more than a length.

After the finish of each race the winning boat sailed a "lap of honour" streaming the victor's pennant on a short course that ran parallel to the Parade, while the band, seated on the Donkey Stand, played the melody of a song that included some mention of the winning boat's name. For example, when Dick Peters won the Nobbies' race in his boat 'Onward', the band played 'Onward Christian Soldiers'.

Some names must have taxed the musicians' ingenuity, but it is said that none of the bandmasters ever failed to think of an appropriate musical tribute.

Prizes were always cash.

After the competitors had eaten the very substantial high tea that was provided, the festivities came to an end with childrens' games and dancing on the Green, an area behind the Parade houses that has since disappeared under housing development.

The last regatta was held in 1914 and, although attempts were made in later years to revive the Event, it was never held again in its traditional form.

In the later nineteen-thirties working out of Parkgate became increasingly difficult, and the fishermen began to moor their boats at Heswall or Thurstaston, commuting to these anchorages in vans. After the Second World War conditions became so difficult that no young men entered the trade. Numbers of fishermen fell rapidly until today no more than a handful remain to tell of their lives and work.

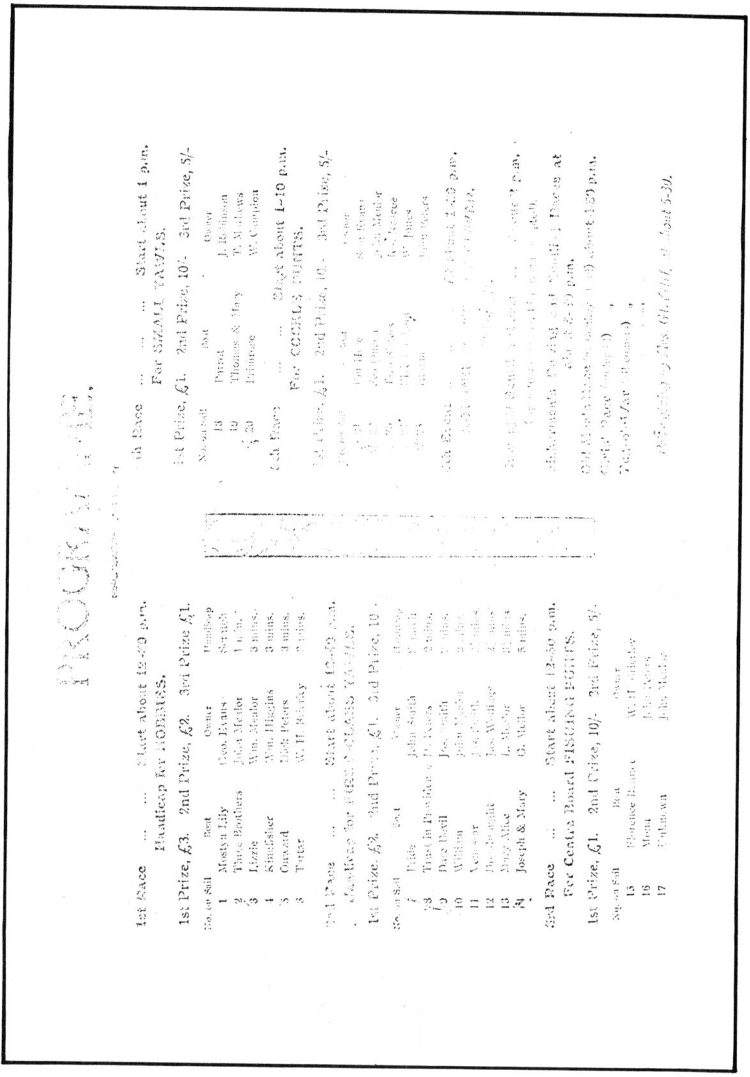

PROGRA[illegible]ME.

1st Race ... ... Start about 12-20 p.m.
Handicap for HOBBIES.

1st Prize, £3. 2nd Prize, £2. 3rd Prize £1.

No. on Sail	Boat	Owner	Handicap
1	Mostyn Lily	Geo. Evans	Scratch
2	Three Brothers	John Mellor	1 min.
3	Lizzie	Wm. Mealor	3 mins.
4	Kingfisher	Wm. Higgins	3 mins.
5	Onward	Dick Peters	3 mins.
6	Tartar	W. H. [illegible]	[illegible] mins.

2nd Race ... ... Start about 12-40 p.m.
Handicap for FIRST-CLASS YAWLS.

1st Prize, £2. 2nd Prize, £1. 3rd Prize, 10/-

No. on Sail	Boat	Owner	Handicap
7	Pride	John Smith	Scratch
8	Trust in Providence	P. Peters	2 mins.
9	Dare Devil	Jos. Smith	[illegible] mins.
10	William	John Mealor	[illegible] mins.
11	[illegible]	Jas. Smith	[illegible] mins.
12	Dreadnaught	Jas. Wedlake	[illegible] mins.
13	Mary Alice	L. Mellor	[illegible] mins.
14	Joseph & Mary	G. Mellor	5 mins.

3rd Race ... ... Start about 12-50 p.m.
For Centre Board FISHING PUNTS.

1st Prize, £1. 2nd Prize, 10/- 3rd Prize, 5/-

No. on Sail	Boat	Owner
15	Florence [illegible]	W. H. Grierley
16	Mona	John Peters
17	Unknown	John Mealor

[illegible]th Race ... ... Start about 1 p.m.
For SMALL YAWLS.

1st Prize, £1. 2nd Prize, 10/- 3rd Prize, 5/-

No. on Sail	Boat	Owner
18	Parrot	J. Robinson
19	Thomas & Mary	T. Mathews
20	Primrose	W. Campion

[illegible]th Race ... ... Start about 1-10 p.m.
For COCKLE PUNTS.

1st Prize, £1. 2nd Prize, 10/- 3rd Prize, 5/-

No. on Sail	Boat	Owner
21	[illegible]	[illegible] Evans
[illegible]	[illegible]	John Mellor
[illegible]	[illegible]	[illegible]
[illegible]	[illegible]	W. Jones
[illegible]	[illegible]	John Peters

[illegible]th Event ... ... [illegible] about 1-20 p.m.
[illegible]

[illegible] about [illegible] p.m.
[illegible]

[illegible]ishermen's [illegible] Races at [illegible] p.m.

Old Men's Race [illegible] about 4-30 p.m.
Girls' Race [illegible] ,,
Tug-o'-War [illegible] ,,

[illegible] Mrs. Gl. [illegible] about 5-30.

Programme of last Parkgate Fishermen's Regatta. (Held in 1914). (Author's Collection).

APPENDIX B

The Colliery

Even in its present tumbledown state the old mine quay, close to the 'Harp' inn, is an impressive relic of an important and fascinating aspect of Neston history.

Built in the middle of the eighteenth century to serve the Denhall colliery at a time when coastwise shipping offered the only economical means of carrying bulk goods, the Quay was also a suitable place from which to export the coal to Ireland and the Isle of Man.

Remains of the old mine quay at Denhall. (Kind permission of Messrs E.T.W. Dennis and Sons Ltd.).

Mining activity in the district was based on an outlier of the North Wales Coalfield that occupies a small area to the south of Neston.

The Stanley Family of Hooton opened the first colliery about 1760, and imported miners from Lancashire, Staffordshire and North Wales to work it.

At their greatest extent, the main tunnels ran for more than a mile under the estuary. Although this mine was worked for almost half a century, no information appears to be available concerning the quality or quantity of coal extracted. It did, however, possess one feature of special interest: the coal was carried along the main tunnels to the bottom of the shaft by means of underground canals.

Mortimer in his book "The History of The Hundred of Wirral" (1847) stated that there were two canals, one at a depth of sixty yards and the other at ninety-four yards below the surface.

The Neston Colliery – from a water colour by Arthur Suker, dated 1875. (Courtesy Williamson Art Gallery).

Almost certainly, the barges used were similar to the so-called 'starvationers' that were built at that time for the canals in the Worsley mines. Long, narrow, shallow and flat-bottomed with exposed ribs that earned them their peculiar nickname, all boats in the Denhall pit carried four baskets containing four hundred weights each — a sort of eighteenth century container system. Four or five boats were roped together in a train, and then propelled along the canals by miners who lay with their backs placed across the boats' gunwales, and then "walked" along the roof, taking the barges with them. As might be expected, progress was slow: Mortimer mentioned a speed of a mile an hour.

Early in the nineteenth century the Stanleys must have lost interest in mining because the following advertisement appeared in "The Courant" of 29th August, 1812:

"To be let for any term not exceeding 30 years. Ness Colliery, close to the River Dee, where coals are shipped off an extensive and convenient quay for Ireland, North and South Wales, and the Isle of

Man. Together with a farm of about 90 statute acres etc., adjoining the works etc.

The coal consists of three veins of 6, 5 and 7 feet respectively, as well as one of two feet. Under the last there is a seam of excellent fire clay etc. etc.

For further particular application should be made to Mr. Ashurst of Puddington."

There seems to have been a shortage of suitable applicants because, shortly afterwards, the mine closed.

A few years later another mine was sunk closer to Neston. Most of the output was steam coal, but a certain amount of household coal was produced from one of the seams, "The King Seam". During the early part of its existence the bulk of the coal was exported from the same quay that had served the Denhall mine. In 1866, however the opening of the Hooton to Parkgate railway line linked the mine with the national railway system and in the years that followed the railway companies became the main customers for the steam coal.

Working conditions in the mine were unpleasant. In his book "The Wirral Peninsula" Norman Ellison commented that a visit he made to the Ness Colliery when he was a boy was enough to convince him that his future did not lie in mining. Almost inevitably in a pit where the tunnels ran out under an estuary, the workings were subject to heavy water seepage, and continuous pumping was necessary to

Photograph of Ness Mine c.1910. (Courtesy Ian Boumphrey).

prevent flooding. The small additional allowance paid to those miners who were obliged to work crouching in icy water can hardly have compensated for the misery involved.

Another unpleasant feature of the mine, particularly before The First World War, was the vermin that infested the workings. Mice and cockroaches were the miners' ever-present companions. One of the first lessons every new man learnt was to carry his sandwiches in a tin box; if he carried them in a cloth or wrapped in paper they would be eaten before his break arrived.

The presence of these pests seems to have been connected with the use of pit ponies in the mine. The warmth of the underground stables and the food and water provided for the animals may have fostered the conditions that allowed vermin to thrive. Certain it is that when the ponies were replaced by machinery, about 1916, the vermin level fell rapidly.

Although no large scale disaster seems to have occurred at the Ness pit, it was, like most coal mines, a dangerous place. Over the years a number of men were killed in rock falls, and there was the ever-present threat posed by pockets of methane gas. A more unusual hazard was presented by the many fossilised trees encountered in the mine. "We would tunnel right through them, and you could see the

Scene in Ness Colliery. (Author's Collection).

rings in the roof of the tunnel", explained one former miner. "Sometimes the whole tree would drop out of the roof, like a pillar of stone. There were a few accidents caused that way".

The mine was finally closed because it could not be operated economically. On several occasions the company that worked it went into voluntary liquidation, to be replaced by another company which, in turn, was obliged to submit to liquidation. Thus, "Neston Colliery Ltd." was succeeded by "Wirral Colliery Ltd." which in due course, was replaced by "Wirral Colliery (1915) Ltd.". The problem was not caused by the high cost of operating the pit. Indeed, operating costs appear to have been below average: at no point was the mine deeper than three hundred feet; the seams were fairly thick and, therefore, easy to work; and by selling much of the coal at the pithead to the railways, transport cost could be reduced to a minimum. The main difficulty was that of selling the steam coal, the bulk of the output, at a price which covered the cost of its production. The household coal could be sold on the Wirral Peninsula at a profit, but the force of competition from other collieries ensured that the large consumers, to whom steam coal might be sold, could buy the coal at a price that frequently fell below the cost of production.

In 1916 the mine was taken into public ownership and, as a maximum production was needed for the war effort, operations were maintained with the aid of government subsidies.

The last shift, 12 March, 1927. (Courtesy Ian Boumphrey).

In 1919 the mine was returned to the ownership of Wirral Colliery (1915) Ltd. Almost at once, the company began to experience the same difficulties that had dogged its predecessors before the war. An attempt was made to save the situation by buying the rights to exploit a new, good-quality, seam that lay under a neighbouring farmer's fields, but negotiations broke down over terms. The Company struggled on until 1927 and then submitted to the inevitable liquidation. There being no investors willing to form another company, the mine was finally closed, the last shift being worked on 12th March, 1927.

The colliery was the biggest single employer of labour in the district, and its closure caused a serious local unemployment problem. The "Register of Mines" for 1926 recorded a hundred and eleven men as being employed underground, and thirty-seven on the surface. Although some men moved out of the area to find work in other mines, unemployment remained a problem until the outbreak of the Second World War created a demand for manpower in the services and in war work.

APPENDIX C

Neston Female Friendly Society

On the first Thursday of every June Neston echoes to the sound of Festival as the ladies of the local Female Friendly Society walk in procession through the town, drawing sightseers in their hundreds from the surrounding district.

Theirs is an organisation with a claim to distinction. Formed in 1814 as a means of mutual self-help for women, it was the first female friendly society in the country. By paying regular subscriptions the members were able to establish and maintain a fund, from which they could claim assistance in times of financial difficulty, such as sickness and old age.

Of course, friendly societies had existed long before 1814 — there is one society in existence that can trace its origins to the mid-sixteenth century — the novelty lay in the idea of women having enough imagination and enterprise to band together for any purpose, let alone for a cause as important as mutual financial support.

In the early nineteenth century, when official assistance for the penniless involved either the stigma of parish relief or the humiliation of the workhouse, the society was an innovation that enabled ordinary women to achieve a measure of dignity that had previously been denied them.

The original idea seems to have been that of the vicar, Prebendary Thomas Ward. An enlightened man with views well in advance of his time and an impressive record in local social work, Ward was careful to limit his participation to calling an inaugural meeting and helping to draft the society's rules before leaving the ladies to conduct their own affairs.

Those present at that first meeting defined the objective of the proposed society as being "for raising a fund by voluntary subscription, towards the support of the old, sick, lame, and infirm members thereof".

The news of this new type of society travelled rapidly, and so many female friendly societies sprang up on the course of the next thirty years that by 1850 there were few places of any size without one. An elaborate system of correspondence developed between the societies by means of which problems were discussed and ideas exchanged.

Curiously enough, although the formation of the Society may be regarded as an early step along the road leading to women's emancipation, the rules have always stipulated that the Secretary shall be a man. Almost certainly, this was because in the early nineteenth century few women would have had the sort of business experience needed to fill the post. Even so, the founders made sure that the appointment would not expose them to the possibility of a male take-over. The same rule which provides for the appointment of a male secretary continues: "The Secretary shall, on all occasions, in the execution of his office, act under the superintendence, control and direction of the Committee of Management".

From the beginning, the Society's annual Anniversary Walk became an occasion for a local holiday, when schools were closed, buildings were draped with bunting, and all roads in Neston led to the High Street. Over the years it has become the day when all exiled Nestonians who can do so return to their home town to renew old acquaintances and associations.

"On the first day of June," state the original rules that now hang framed and faded in the Town Hall, "the members shall meet and walk in orderly procession to Church when an appropriate sermon shall be preached and at four in the evening of the same day, the members shall meet again when they shall drink tea together."

Changed to the first Thursday in June in 1815, time has shown the choice of day to have been a good one: "Ladies Day" weather is almost invariably fine.

The founders did not, however, forget that the Society was all about economics. To forestall the possibility of members impoverishing themselves in some sort of unofficial internecine,

Ladies Club 1906. Note the clock in the Tower Building. This was removed about 1910 because its chiming had clashed with that of the Church Clock. (Courtesy Ian Boumphrey).

dress competition on the big day, the rules also stipulated that the members shall "not be otherwise dressed on that day than in stuff, printed linen, and cotton gowns on forfeiture of one shilling to the box".

Known affectionately as "The Ladies Club", the Society has for long been the subject of considerable local pride. Writing in praise of his town towards the end of the last century Neston poet James Stonehouse penned the following lines:

". . . a famous club
That female thrift imposes,
That marches through the town with flags,
A band and lovely posies,
There matrons mix with pretty girls,
With doctors and with clergy,
If these don't stir your heart's delight
There's nought on earth can urge ye."

As poetry the lines may leave something to be desired, but the pride is unmistakable.

For an institution that generates so much local pride, the Society's affairs have remained remarkably free from controversy.

There was just one unfortunate incident, in 1864. The Committee decided that the town band was not playing well enough to lead the fiftieth Anniversary Walk, and invited the band of the Chester Volunteers to do so.

It was a decision that rocked the town to its foundations, dividing the population into pro and anti Committee factions and setting neighbour against neighbour.

The members of the band wasted little time on argument. For them it was an insult that demanded action, not words. On the day of the Walk they waited until the members of the Society were comfortably seated in Church and the service had begun and then formed up under the east window and launched into a cacophonous march. So loud was the noise that it brought the vicar to a halt in mid-sentence and prevented him from continuing. It was not until the Rector of Heswall, Mark Coxon, who was visiting Neston for the occasion, came out to remonstrate with them that they agreed to stop playing.

Although the band's action was regarded as nothing less than scandalous, as a protest it was markedly effective. Never again, as long as Neston could muster a town band, were outsiders invited to play for the Walk, and never again was the Society troubled by that sort of controversy.

On the only other occasion that a similar situation arose the matter was resolved by negotiation and sweet reason. For 112 years the official celebrations ended with country dancing to music provided by the brass band that played for the procession in the afternoon, but in 1926 a number of younger members asked the Committee to introduce modern dancing.

Bearing in mind the 1864 experience, the Committee asked the Secretary, Dick Wharam, to ascertain the attitude of the band to the proposed change before making a decision. To the surprise of many, the bandsmen were delighted with the proposal, which offered them the opportunity of enjoying the delights of the Charleston, the Black Bottom and the Foxtrot, while others did the work.

Neston Ladies Club 1909. (Courtesy Ian Boumphrey).

While public interest has tended to centre on the "Ladies Day" walk and Anniversary celebrations, the essential work of the Society — the work of mutual assistance — has continued quietly and efficiently every year since 1814. In return for their subscriptions, members claim sickness pay and maternity benefit whenever they are in need, and a payment is made towards funeral expenses when a member dies.

Until 1948, when the National Health Service was introduced, the Society operated its own health scheme and the local doctors walked in the annual procession as medical officers of the Society. After the government scheme had been implemented the Society discontinued its own scheme and the doctors ceased to take part in the event. There can be no doubt that with the departure of the medical men in their colourful academic robes and tasselled caps the aura of the occasion faded a little.

One of the assurances the Society has always offered its members is that they will receive a decent and proper funeral. In the nineteenth century, and for much of this century, when a pauper's funeral was a very real and humiliating prospect for many people, such an assurance was an important consideration.

Not only does the Society make a payment towards the cost of the funeral, it requires its members to honour their dead in their own traditional manner. As the coffin is carried from the hearse to the church they silently line both sides of the path, each member holding upright a plain white staff, at the top of which is tied a black crepe ribbon bow. As the coffin leaves the church they again line the path in the same manner. It is a simple and yet strangely moving tribute. A monarch could not ask to be buried with greater dignity.

It is, however, the colourful Anniversary Walk that keeps the Society in the public eye and mind. Led by a band hired for the occasion — sadly there is now no local band — the long procession of brightly-dressed women and girls makes its way down the High Street to the Parish Church. In their hands they carry the same white staves that they carry at funerals, but instead of black crepe they are garlanded with flowers, and ribbons.

Traditionally the flowers are gathered from the member's own gardens. Red paeonies, which are at their best in the Neston area during the early part of June, have become such a feature of the occasion that they are known locally as "Ladies Day Flowers".

Before the procession two stalwarts bear the society's seven foot square banner with its motif of clasped hands, and text from St. Paul's letter to the Galatians, "Bear Ye One Another's Burdens".

Over the course of the years successive banners have deteriorated and been replaced, and there have been some variations in the design.

A particularly interesting one was commissioned to mark Queen Victoria's Diamond Jubilee. It bore a portrait of the Queen, with the dates 1837-1897, and the legend "Long May She Reign in her People's Hearts". Economy being the watch-word of the Society, this banner remained in use well into the reign of Edward VII.

Like many other ancient institutions, the Society has its mystery. Carried high towards the front of the procession is "The Dispensation", a staff that is surmounted by the Society's badge, and two large garlands. Both the origin of the Dispensation itself and its name have been lost in the mists of time. Of the many theories that have been advanced, the most likely seems to be that the Society's original charter was once carried in a cylinder that was attached to the staff. But why "Dispensation"?

The Mayor in his robes and chain of office, members of the local clergy, and many other local dignitaries walk, as the guests of the society.

Neston Ladies Club 1982. (Courtesy David Scott).

Neston Ladies Club 1982. (Courtesy David Scott).

Inside the church the scene is as colourful as that in the High Street, with flowers packed on to every ledge that will hold them. Before taking their seats the members of the Society stand their staves in the umbrella holders at the end of the pews, transforming the aisles into avenues of flowers.

After the service the procession walks to the Town Cross, where a hymn and the National Anthem are sung. The walkers then disperse, to meet a little later for tea.

Sadly, changes have taken place over the years and Ladies Day is not the festival it once was. The advent of reasonably generous holidays for everyone has reduced the importance of the event in the life of the community. Long gone are the pierrot shows that were a popular feature of the Day before the First World War. The dance too, has gone, discontinued for lack of support, and with it the custom of adjourning to the town centre after the official function had finished to dance around the fountain on the Cross until after midnight. Few shops and businesses now close for the day, and even the schools remain open.

Within recent years, however, the Society has assumed an additional importance: it is, once more, unique. All the other female friendly societies in the country have been disbanded, rendered obsolete by the welfare state. Only the ladies of Neston, conscious of their responsibilities as the guardians of a tradition, walk in the footsteps of the pioneers of 1814.

APPENDIX D

The Parkgate Ferries

The first regular ferry service across the Dee Estuary seems to have been established between Parkgate and Flint about 1740.

Before the introduction of the ferry, travellers who wished to cross the Estuary were obliged to use the hazardous so-called "sand roads" at low tide.

The new service seems to have been well patronised because the demand for passage on the route soon exceeded the capacity of the available facilities. In 1786 a correspondent wrote to the editor of "The Chester Chronicle" complaining that the service did not provide for the carriage of animals, and that travellers were obliged to leave their horses behind.

The deficiency was rectified three years later when the following advertisement appeared in "Gore's Liverpool General Advertiser" dated November 5th 1789:

"Parkgate and Flint Ferryboat

Thomas Spencer of the George Inn, Parkgate, and Daniel Jones of the Ship Inn, Flint, respectfully inform those ladies, Gentlemen, and others travelling between the two places, that they have fitted up a large, commodious, Two Mast and Row Boat for the conveyance of Passengers, Horses, Cattle etc., well manned with sober and experienced boatmen.

Passengers will be pleased to enquire for the boat called the "Llenwenny" at either of the above inns or of Margaret Totty of Parkgate."

It was fortunate for the operators that there was no such thing as an Eighteenth Century Trade Description Act, otherwise the reference to "sober and experienced boatmen" might have involved them in legal difficulties.

When two women were drowned in 1799 following the capsize of "The Friends" ferry boat the editor of "The Chester Chronicle" commented:

"The Flint and Parkgate boats have been used to carry too much sail in trying to out-sail each other, to the great danger and terror of the passengers."

Although the boatmen appear to have adopted a more responsible attitude by the time Richard Ayton made the crossing from Flint to Parkgate in 1813, he still found the experience to be far from pleasant.

Built in the early "1920s" "The Boat House" is named after the Ferry Boats. (Author's Collection).

Recording the journey in his book "A Voyage Round Great Britain" he wrote:

"A packet boat sails regularly, when the tide permits, from Flint to the opposite shore, and in this we took our passage, together with a crowd of other passengers, being packed and crammed into one's place with as little regard for our ease in such a state of stowage as though we had been dead cargo. It was proposed to us, as some comfort, that there was quite as much room on the present occasion as we should have found on any other day, and that nobody had ever made the passage with less reason to grumble. There are but two boats, and they can ply for only two hours of each flood; it is necessary, therefore to load; them at once, with as many as will consent to go together."

At that time the Parkgate landing place was at the Ferry House Inn, which stood on the site now occupied by the Boathouse Restaurant, and it was owned by a Mr J. Davies.

It was in Davies' time that an abortive attempt was made to modernise the ferry. An advertisement in the "Liverpool Mercury" dated 30th June 1817, announced that a new steam packet, "The Ancient Briton," had begun sailing between Parkgate and Bagillt, making three round passages on each tide.

A new pier was built at Parkgate and a good landing place at Bagillt. Travellers bound for Liverpool were carried by coach to Tranmere to meet a Mr. Ball's new steam boat "The Regulator".

This co-ordinated service did not last for long. "The Regulator" sank in a gale in January 1818, "The Ancient Briton" was sold to new owners on the Mersey, and once more, the Dee crossings were made by sailing boats only.

The Parkgate-Bagillt Ferry continued to operate until 1864. By that time it had lost so much traffic to the new circuitous but reliable railway route between North Wales and Wirral that when the then proprietor, Thomas Johnson, was drowned in trying to land from the ferry boat in a heavy swell, the service was allowed to lapse for lack of interest.

APPENDIX E

Ness Gardens

The rise of Ness Gardens to a status approaching that of a national institution has been rapid. Founded in 1898 — a mere yesterday in gardening terms — the Gardens have become a place of pilgrimage for garden-lovers from all parts of Britain and abroad.

For some the Heather Garden, unparallelled in this country and recognised as one of the finest in the world, is the main attraction. Others linger over the magnificent collection of rhododendrons, or in the Rock Gardens, or by one of the many other features.

The Rock Garden, Ness Gardens. (Courtesy the Director, Ness Gardens).

Most people, however, find their chief delight in the Gardens as a whole rather than in one particular feature. For them every turn in the path opens a new vista to please: vistas of trees and grass, shrubs and flowers, or rocks and water; vistas that change with the light and the seasons, so that no matter how often the visitor returns nothing is ever quite the same as on previous occasions.

At Ness the qualities of a gardeners' garden and the virtues of an ornamental pleasure garden have been reconciled to an extent that is rarely seen elsewhere.

Ness Gardens, or to be correct, the University of Liverpool Botanic Gardens, Ness, were established at the turn of the century by wealthy Liverpool cotton broker Arthur Bulley in the grounds of his new house 'Mickwell Brow'.

Situated on a low hill commanding a panoramic view of the Dee Estuary and the Clwydian Mountains, the sixty acre site afforded a number of natural advantages, including a variety of soils, a south-facing slope which, with its somewhat higher temperatures increased the range of plants that might be cultlivated, and the undulating nature of the ground which offered possibilities for the future creation of vistas.

Early development was, however, restricted by the north-west gales that blow in from the Irish Sea. Belts of trees were planted to protect the site, and the first ornamental features were laid out in, and confined to, the more sheltered parts of the estate.

Arthur Bulley's influence on British gardening has been considerable. As an enthusiastic naturalist, he was interested in the "acclimatisation" of plants from abroad, and from 1904 until the beginning of the Second World War he spent a considerable fortune financing expeditions by plant collectors such as George Forrest, Frank Kingdom-Ward and Clarence Elliott. From all parts of the globe, but from Asia in particular, they brought back thousands of specimens.

Many flowers and shrubs now seen in gardens throughout the country were first imported via Ness. Among them are some 200 to 300 varieties of rhododendrons, the several varieties of Himalayan Cowslip, the brilliantly-coloured lily-of-the-valley tree (pieris formosa forestii). Some of the plants raised from the original imported seeds may still be seen flourishing at Ness.

Not that traditional English Garden flowers have been neglected. Shakespearian devotees would have no trouble in finding the various flowers in Ophelia's bouquet — rosemary, pansy, fennel, columbine, rue, daisy and violet — or the actual variety of rose about which Shakespeare and his contemporaries were so fond of writing — Fair Rosamund's Rose — the original Rose of England.

Apparently somewhat uneasy at the responsibility of having (in his own words to Doctor Yeoman), ". . . . more money than the heart of man could desire," Arthur Bulley searched for ways in which he could share his good fortune with others, and allowing the public free access to his gardens throughout the year was just one of the many ways that he chose to do so. "A walk to Bulley's Gardens" soon became a popular outing for local residents.

In terms of local history it is interesting to note that the site was a favourite local picnic spot long before Bulley's time. It was also used

Arthur Kilpin Bulley. (Courtesy the Director, Ness Gardens).

as an occasional meeting place for Methodist camp services and in his "Little Neston Methodist Church Centenary History" Edward Hilditch records the story of a woman who became so incensed by a preacher who was denouncing wickedness that she was unable to contain herself. "Yes, wicked Ness", she shouted, "but the people at Burton and Puddington are just as wicked".

Arthur Bulley died in 1942 and in 1948 his daughter, Miss A.L. Bulley, presented the whole estate, together with a handsome endownment, to the University of Liverpool, "as a practical and fitting tribute to the memory of her father." A condition of the gift was that the policy of opening the grounds to the public should be continued.

During the war years, with staff much reduced, development was halted. Almost single-handed, head gardener, Josiah Hope tended to the essential tasks which needed to be done if the Gardens were to flourish again after the War. A man who started work at Ness in 1911 and never wholly retired until his death in 1970 at the age of 96, his service to the Gardens is now commemorated by a stone, bearing a plaque, which has been erected among the plants he loved.

One of the first post-war developments was the creation of the Heather Garden, when thousands of plants of many varieties were laid out on a particularly suitable south-west slope. Thirty years later the result is spectacular. The coastal climate favours heathers, and varieties which struggle for survival inland have flourished at Ness. At its best in summer when the flowers tumble down the hill in a multi-coloured torrent, it is nothing less than a masterpiece of the gardener's art.

Soon after the present Director of the Gardens, Kenneth Hulme, was appointed in 1956, he decided that the shelter belts of trees had grown to the stage where the original arrangements of features in compartments could be abandoned and The Gardens re-modelled to afford an integral progression from one feature to the next.

The programme of development has continued since it was initiated and still it goes on. The work has included the acquisition of additional land, the landscaping of the Gardens to create distant vistas in which trees and shrubs are used to frame the great bulk of Moel Fammau, rising above the ridge of the Clwydian Mountains across the Estuary, the construction of steps, walls and terraces, and the creation of the Water, Herb and Native Plant Gardens.

Unspectacular as it is when compared to the ornamental features, the Native Plant Collection is a conservation project that alone would establish Ness as an important botanical centre. The creation of the Collection in 1978 has helped to safeguard the continued existence of many British wild plants that had become endangered species, and affords visitors to the Gardens the opportunity to inspect these rare species.

The tufted saxifrage, for example, had been reduced to just four plants in England and Wales growing together on a narrow ledge in Snowdonia. One step by a climber could have destroyed them. Now the species is safe. Seeds from the four plants grown at Ness have enabled more specimens to be returned to the mountains, given the Gardens a stock, and allowed a reserve of 10,000 seeds to be created at Kew.

At present some 150 species are protected in the Native Plant Garden but, as might be expected, the position concerning endangered plants is continually reviewed and others will be added as the need arises.

Even a financial crisis failed to stop the outward surge of development at Ness. When the estate was presented to the University of Liverpool in 1948 the interest on the £75,000 endowment which accompanied it was more than enough to meet all routine expenses, but by 1970 costs and inflation had risen to the point where income from the endowment met only ten per cent of such expenses, leaving the other ninety per cent and the cost of new works to be met by the University.

Although the steadily-increasing burden was eased by the generous contributions made by "The Friends of Ness Gardens," a society formed in 1962 for the purpose of providing improvement and amenities that could not be provided by the University, by 1979 it had become clear that the policy of allowing the public free entry to the ground could not be maintained.

Miss Bulley agreed to change the terms of her gift to allow an administrative charge to be made and, at Easter 1980, a modest entry fee was introduced. The effect on admission was immediate. In twelve months that followed the number of visitors fell from the 80,000 of the previous twelve months to 60,000.

Despite this fall in the number of visitors and the doubts it raised about the financial future of the Gardens, the decision was taken to proceed with plans for the construction of a Visitor Centre. Work was begun in the autumn of 1980, and the building was completed in April, 1981. The first Visitor Centre to be purpose-built in any English Botanic Gardens, it comprised an audio-visual room, where slide sequences with taped commentaries are presented at set times during the day, and a 150 seat lecture theatre.

In 1984 the Visitor Centre was completed when a conservatory was opened. Built with the aid of a handsome grant from The English Tourist Board, the conservatory serves as a concourse area for people attending meetings at the Centre.

Since the completion of the Centre the number of visitors has increased steadily. Whether there is a direct relationship between the two is a matter for conjecture, but it is certain that the audio-visual shows are popular, leaders of organised parties appreciate the use of the Lecture Theatre, and the horticulture courses which are organised jointly by the University and the W.E.A. have become better attended since the Centre became available.

And still development continues. Indefatigable in their endless quest for beauty, Ken Hulme and his staff work as if perfection were attainable.

BIBLIOGRAPHY

Beck, John "*Tudor Cheshire*" (1969).
"*Birkenhead News*" – Various issues.
Bu'Lock J.D. "*Pre.Conquest Chesire 383-1066*" (1972).
"*Chester Chronicle*" – Various issues.
Borough of Ellesmere Port and Neston "*Official Handbook*" (1981).
Ellison Norman "*The Wirral Peninsula*" (1955).
Gamlin, Hilda "*Twixt Mersey and Dee*" (1898).
H.M.S.O. "*Census for England and Wales – County of Chester – 1801-1971*" (Every tenth year, except 1941).
Hewitt, H.J. "*Cheshire under the Three Edwards*" (1967).
Hilditch, E. "*Little Methodist Church, Centenary History*" (1972).
Mercer, W.B. "*A Survey of the Argriculture of Cheshire*" (1963).
Mortimer William "*History of the Hundred of Wirral*" (1847).
Neston Parish Church Registers.
Neston Parish Magazine Supplement (November 1925).
Neston Urban District Council "An Outline for Neston Urban District" (1946).
Place, Geoffrey "*Neston Town Trail*" (1983).
Place, Geoffrey "*This is Parkgate*" (1979).
Sulley, Philip "*The Hundred of Wirral*" (1889).
Sylvester D. and Nulty G. "*The Historical Atlas of Cheshire*" (1958).
D.M. Woodward "*The trade of the Elizabethan Chester*" (1970).

OTHER COUNTYVISE TITLES